-/20

PRAISE FOR
LIVE LOVE NOW

If you are the parent or grandparent of a preteen or teen, or if you have any interaction at all with teens or tweens, you need to read this book. It is packed with powerful reminders of how our words, actions, attitudes, and availability (or lack thereof) leave indelible marks on the next generation. I was inspired, convicted, and challenged by Rachel's gentle message of how to guide, encourage, and impact young adults to live with less stress and more joy. I took away many practical applications to immediately implement in our home and parenting.

CRYSTAL PAINE, *New York Times* bestselling author, podcaster, and founder of MoneySavingMom.com

In a world where stress and burnout make it so hard for parents and children to meaningfully connect, *Live Love Now* is a ray of hope. It's a book that will empower readers to adapt to the new realities of parenting and build strong relationships with the young people in their lives where they model what they want to teach them.

ARIANNA HUFFINGTON, founder and CEO of Thrive Global

Rachel Macy Stafford is unmatched in finding the beauty within the ordinary moments in life. In her newest book, *Live Love Now*, she not only shares the profound benefit of authentically connecting with our children, but she also provides specific ideas on living into it. If you hope to have an enduring, life-giving relationship with the young people in your life, read this book. You'll be grateful you did—and so will the kids you love.

JOHN O'LEARY, host of the *Live Inspired Podcast* and bestselling author of *On Fire*

Live Love Now is a gorgeous manual for how to rescue yourself, your family, and your kid from the malaise of modern parenting. You'll tear up as you feel the truth of it and feel relief at having a clear way forward. This is a must-read for all parents.

JULIE LYTHCOTT-HAIMS, *New York Times* bestselling author of *How to Raise an Adult*

Through heartfelt and authentic life experiences, Rachel Macy Stafford shows that adults and children can learn and grow together, and that perfection is not required to raise healthy and capable young adults. *Live Love Now* will help you become a truth-teller, encourager, and guide to children, helping them find meaning and purpose for themselves instead of trying to fit into roles society tries to nudge them into. In this book, Rachel shares inspiring stories, strategies that value your own experiences, and ways to apply new concepts to the shifting challenges of raising and educating children in a high-pressured world.

MARILYN PRICE-MITCHELL, PhD, developmental psychologist, author of *Tomorrow's Change Makers*, and founder of Roots of Action

In *Live Love Now*, Rachel Macy Stafford provides heartfelt and astute guidance for navigating the places where ourselves and our kids' selves rub up against each other, and she challenges us to put aside our own paradigms—our baggage, if you will—in order to see more clearly the gifts of our children, and to celebrate and nurture those gifts. This is a parenting book like no other you've read. It's a must-read for parents of kids of all ages.

DR. SHEFALI TSABARY, clinical psychologist and *New York Times* bestselling author

Rachel's transparent and practical insights inspire us to do just what the title promises: LIVE LOVE NOW. Reading this book reminded me, yet again, why hers is one of the most important voices of our day.

JOSHUA BECKER, founder of Becoming Minimalist

Loving our kids well as they grow up has more to do with *who they are* than with *who we want them to be*. While many parenting books counsel us on how we can get our kids to meet *our* expectations, Rachel Macy Stafford asks us to take a different approach—to see our kids for who they were created to be, lay down our expectations of who we think they need to become, and come alongside them as guides and companions on their unique journeys.

AMY MCCREADY, founder of Positive Parenting
Solutions and author of *The "Me, Me, Me"*
Epidemic: A Step-by-Step Guide to Raising Capable,
Grateful Kids in an Over-Entitled World

In *Live Love Now,* Rachel Macy Stafford does what she does best: she lovingly encourages, guides, and challenges us to be better than we've been. Through stories, reflections, and tangible tools rooted in love and solidarity, Rachel helps us find our way through the difficulties of parenting without shaming us in process. Read this book and let its kindness pour over you. Take its lessons and make your world a healthier place. Because of Rachel, I know that a better way to love and practice presence is possible.

KAITLIN B CURTICE, author of *Glory Happening* and
Native: Identity, Belonging, and Rediscovering God

We all want to raise confident, resilient teens, but in today's world, it isn't easy. This book has answers, offering guidance to help parents be the anchors and touchstones our teens need to make their way through the sometimes-stormy seas of adolescence. I hope every parent keeps a copy on their nightstand.

SUSAN STIFFELMAN, MFT, author of *Parenting with*
Presence and *Parenting without Power Struggles*

Rachel Macy Stafford has an incredible capacity to turn ordinary words into soul-fulfilling inspiration, and *Live Love Now* is a gift to parents of teens everywhere. Stafford leans in to her own vulnerability to reach her readers right where they are: in the thick of parenting teens through what can only be described as a time of high stress and anxiety. Stafford reminds us that simple changes often yield positive results. Her focus on acceptance, encouragement, and gentle guidance reminds parents to step away from judgment (their own and those of others) and meet their teens where they are in their journey through adolescence. This is a book I will recommend over and over again.

KATIE HURLEY, LCSW, author of *No More Mean Girls* and *The Happy Kid Handbook*

Imagine if we gave our children what they crave above all else: our attention and a clear picture of who they really are. In *Live Love Now*, Rachel Macy Stafford provides us the road map to do just that! She offers not just advice, but scripts and mantras for changing our parenting so we see the children in front of us: kids desperate to be seen and heard for who they are. This book is a guide, a practical and accessible manual any parent can follow.

JESSICA LAHEY, author of *The Gift of Failure: How the Best Parents Learn to Let Go So Their Children Can Succeed*

LIVE LOVE NOW

RELIEVE THE PRESSURE AND FIND REAL
CONNECTION WITH OUR KIDS

Rachel Macy Stafford

ZONDERVAN
BOOKS

ZONDERVAN BOOKS

Live Love Now
Copyright © 2020 by Rachel Macy Stafford

Requests for information should be addressed to:
Zondervan, *3900 Sparks Dr. SE, Grand Rapids, Michigan 49546*

Zondervan titles may be purchased in bulk for educational, business, fundraising, or sales promotional use. For information, please email SpecialMarkets@Zondervan.com.

ISBN 978-0-310-35864-0 (hardcover)

ISBN 978-0-310-35867-1 (international trade paper edition)

ISBN 978-0-310-35866-4 (audio)

ISBN 978-0-310-35865-7 (ebook)

Author is represented by Sandra Bishop, Transatlantic Agency.

Cover design, illustration, and hand-lettering: Jay and Kristi Smith—Juicebox Designs
Back cover image: Amy Paulson
Interior design: Kait Lamphere

Printed in the United States of America

20 21 22 23 24 25 26 27 28 29 30 /LSC/ 15 14 13 12 11 10 9 8 7 6 5 4 3 2 1

To the Wanderers, Noticers, and Dreamers
I've met in classrooms and on hillsides who led me to hope

To my beloved Wanderer and Noticer, Natalie and Avery,
who led me back to my Dreamer

To everyone willing to go where love leads

CONTENTS

PART 3: Be a Guide, Not a Half-Listener

THE TRUTH IS THE BEGINNING

I sit in my car in the middle school parking lot. I dig into my bag until I reach the massive stack of index cards. I hold them carefully in my hands, regarding them as cherished gifts, just as I told the students I would.

Even before I put my key in the ignition, I read the cards. The realities of today's teenage world, written in No. 2 pencil, bring me to tears. I realize I am holding my breath.

I had asked a simple question: *If you could give your parents or the world* one *message, what would it be?*

The students' responses are gold, relaying wisdom and insight far beyond their years. Yet sadly, almost every nugget of truth is wrapped in stress, anxiety, and pain far beyond what most adults would expect.

Some might wonder how an outsider talking about her journey to becoming an author is able to extract such deep truths and weighty insights from middle school students.

Maybe it's the special education teacher in me who spent a decade connecting with young people ranging from kindergarten to twelfth grade who had emotional and behavioral problems.

Maybe it's the dreamer in me who speaks to students right

where they are, tapping into their loftiest aspirations with no judgment or limitations.

Maybe it's the flawed but loving mother in me, admitting my greatest parenting mistakes in the same breath with which I describe the limitless love I have for my children.

Maybe it's because I see myself in them—nervous, uncertain, awkward, but showing up anyway, flawed and full of hope.

Or maybe it's because they see themselves in me—a recovering, tech-tethered, perfectionistic control freak who is determined to resist the highly pressured, barely breathing way of life our society glorifies.

I think, though, it's simply because I admitted I didn't know everything.

"You are an untapped resource," I said. "We adults can learn as much from you as you can from us. And right now, many of us feel like we are failing you."

That was the moment they sat up straighter, leaned in closer, and looked me straight in the eyes.

If you could give your parents or the world one message, what would it be? I repeated the question as I distributed the blank index cards. Pencils began moving rapidly, as if every student had just been waiting for someone to ask.

A few minutes later, while collecting the completed cards, I saw lines filled to capacity, and I knew one thing for sure: in order to receive such honest, heart-wrenching, truthful feedback, I had to be vulnerable first. I had to show the students I am human and give them the space and acceptance to be human too.

Acceptance is where connection forms.

It's in the light of realness—acceptance and truth—that we find hope in our relationships. It might not feel like any kind of hope we've ever felt before. It's messy and awkward, but it's real. And it's strong enough to break down barriers so we can talk about hard things.

The first time I experienced this type of authentic, unifying connection was with my daughter Natalie. At a young age, she began asking me for "Talk Time." This sacred, ten-minute bedtime ritual always began with the same request.

"Tell me something bad that happened in the world today, Mama."

Natalie would then pull her pink daisy blanket up to her chin and add, "I am not scared."

Something told me that if Natalie did not receive the truth from me, this inquisitive girl would search for it in other ways. So, I'd take a deep breath and give Natalie small bits of truth about the realities of the world in words she could understand. Part of me feared these truths would be the end of her innocence, forever tainting her perception to a hopeless gray hue. But every unfiltered glimpse I offered was met by a spark in my child's eyes, indicating to me that even at a young age, Natalie sensed her purpose in the world would be found somewhere in the mess.

Later, when Natalie was seven, I found myself in a dark, depleted, and distracted state. As my world crumbled and my joy disappeared, it was she who constantly took the brunt of my anger, frustration, hopelessness, and stress.

Once, after I harshly blamed her for her little sister's slip on a library book placed on the stairs, Natalie ran to her bedroom. I quietly opened the door to find her with her daisy blanket pulled up to her chin. Remembering the brave question she'd repeatedly asked me at age four, I admitted an ugly truth about myself—a truth I'd never told a soul.

"Natalie, I am mean to myself inside, and I take it out on you," I whispered, my voice quivering with pain. "I'm so sorry. I don't know how, but I pray I can change. I am determined to try."

Natalie did not cry or look afraid. She looked unmistakably hopeful.

The truth was not the end; it was the beginning.

Those moments, when I realized I could be transparent with my children about my missteps and struggles, gave launch to an eight-year journey to uncover and overcome obstacles that were sabotaging my peace, my relationships, my health, my joy, and my purpose. It's taken a lot of hard work, and I don't pretend to have it all figured out, but I am beyond grateful for the breakthroughs I've made as a parent and as a human being over these past years.

Each breakthrough came after I took an honest look at what was causing pain or distance in my relationships, and with a willingness to practice new approaches and find solutions. Many of these breakthroughs are described in detail in my previous books, but they're also relevant here. As we strive to reach and connect authentically with other people in our lives—especially those who look up to us—in order to model authenticity, we have to first deal with our own stuff.

All those years, while I worked to overcome individual and relational obstacles, my family was watching. My children soaked up every intention I made, every strategy I implemented, and every mantra I posted on my bathroom mirror, especially my brown-eyed, wise-beyond-her-years Natalie. And night after night, year after year, she and I would lie down for Talk Time. During those one-on-one nightly talks, she told me things she didn't tell anyone else. I knew Natalie was always honest with me about what she was going through because I had always been honest with her.

As Natalie described the ways she was coping with her own pressures and challenges, I began to hear echoes of the strategies I'd learned throughout my journey—but there was something more. With confidence and courage, Natalie was beginning to cultivate skills for coping with the same stressors that were derailing many of her peers.

She was hardly a perfect child, and today, she's still a teen figuring out her place in the world. But I take heart in knowing that she is resilient and resourceful, kind and assertive, tender and tough. She has bounced back from major letdowns, learned from her mistakes, used her God-given gifts to help others, and refused to let accomplishments, media, or the opinions of others define her worth. I can't take all the credit for the marvelous young woman she's becoming, but I will admit that by practicing acceptance, pursuing peace, and exploring purpose for myself, I'd become a model, a refuge, and a reliable resource for my twenty-first-century child.

One night during Talk Time, exactly a decade after our nightly ritual began, Natalie revealed a deep desire, along with a plan, to go to Africa as soon as possible. It was the place she most often asked about during our heart-to-hearts when she was young. Fulfilling this urging in her heart would require her to push away fear, control, expectation, and comfort.

"I know I'm only fourteen, but I'm determined to do whatever I need to do to travel there."

In that moment, I could not stop the tears. I released what felt like a decade-long exhale that had been waiting for confirmation of a powerful truth: *Perfect parenting is not required to raise resilient, compassionate, and capable adults.* Better off are the kids whose parents are willing to rewrite their job description and admit they are up for the task of learning, discovering, and growing right alongside their children.

As today's parents attempt to raise the first generation of kids battling "technoference," extreme academic pressure, unrealistic expectations, less outdoor time, and more school shootings, it is best if we admit right now that we do not know for certain how to navigate these waters. But if we are willing to live a life anchored by truth, connection, presence, and acceptance, and if we are willing to *live love*, there is great hope.

We have to be vulnerable first. That means our humanness stops being a scary secret right now so we can become respected role models for the young people we love. When our own personal discoveries meet our teen's deepest need to be known, that is where real connection forms—not spotty, superficial, worldly connection, but true, authentic, unifying connection. And that is where a life of peace, purpose, and acceptance can be created, right in the middle of the mayhem and the mess.

The Truth-teller in me is humbled by the thousands of comments I've received from readers and followers who've expressed gratitude for my willingness to share my challenges and discoveries. The Encourager in me is grateful to be able to admit to myself that I'll never have it all figured out, and that the *trying* matters more than the *knowing*. And the Guide in me is compelled to present this book in a useful, instructive format so that it can be a navigational tool and resource on your journey to *Live Love Now*.

Live Love Now is organized into three parts, each identified by the roles I believe adults need to embrace in order to relieve pressure and experience real connection with today's young people: Truth-teller, Encourager, and Guide.

Within these parts, the book addresses the six top stressors our young people face: (1) feeling unseen and unheard, (2) experiencing rejection, (3) the allure and effect of technology usage, (4) lack of life skills, (5) lack of coping skills, and (6) parental and academic pressure.

Each chapter opens with a personal story that led me to an important discovery about how to embrace life and love now—through acceptance, belonging, anchoring, independence, resilience, and worthiness. Each discovery is followed by three examples that illustrate how I used various tools to help my children thrive when they faced specific pressure. For example: Acceptance through Refuge, Acceptance through Reframing, and Acceptance through Respect. Then there are strategies to help you mine your own experiences and compassionately guide the young people you love as they navigate one of the most stressful times in their lives, in an era when the stakes are higher than ever.

To help you stay the course toward connection, each of the three examples concludes with a *Live Love Now* Waypoint, a brief suggestion to help you apply the chapter concept step-by-step, moment-by-moment on an uncharted path. And finally, there are reflection questions to help you further hone your skills as a Truth-teller, Encourager, and Guide.

As you work your way through the book's main concepts and apply them to different life situations, my hope is that you will experience greater awareness and discover effective strategies to navigate any conflict or tension that arises in the life of the young person you love.

I hope the stories of my own mistakes and breakthroughs help you uncover the obstacles that may be sabotaging your health, your happiness, or your relationships. And I hope the principles and strategies on these pages inspire you to begin practicing acceptance, pursuing peace, and exploring purpose for yourself so you can *live love* as a model for the young people in your life.

Be advised, you may uncover things—about yourself and your teen—you don't expect, causing you to wonder if it's too late. I am here to assure you that it is not.

No matter how many obstacles currently stand in your way,
no matter how much damage you feel you have done,
no matter how foreign the teenage world is to you,
no matter how unfamiliar the young people in your life feel
    right now,
teens want you to see them.

And they want you to see yourself in them—nervous, uncertain, awkward, but showing up anyway, flawed and full of hope.

I know, not just because I've read it on hundreds of index cards, but because I've also seen it in the eyes of hundreds of kids.

I'm so grateful for the honest confessions from these anxious teens, as well as the years of ongoing commentary I've read from my online followers, expressing their fears about losing connection with the young people in their lives. Their sincere worries that it is too late, that there's a divide we just can't overcome, are what motivated me to write *Live Love Now*. We may very well be living through an unprecedented time in human history, when division and distraction have us feeling lost and more disconnected than ever. Still, I dare to submit that with small steps and a little self-examination, real connection with the young people in our lives can happen today.

The truth is not the end; it is the beginning.

Let's begin.

PART 1

BE A TRUTH-TELLER, NOT A TASKMASTER

Truth-Tellers . . .

- Share their stories, even the painful and shameful parts, to bring healing to themselves and others.
- Navigate life from a place of authenticity rather than from behind a mask or a façade.
- Show up as themselves, even if it's not who they think the world wants to see.
- Do not rely on external approval for self-worth.
- Make choices by heart, values, and beliefs, not by worldly expectations or demands.
- Lean in when others share their truths.
- Honor others' truths with non-judgmental and compassionate responses.

CHAPTER 1

UNSEEN AND UNHEARD

Being heard is so close to being loved that for the average person they are almost indistinguishable.

—David W. Augsburger, *Caring Enough to Hear and Be Heard*

"This is my dreamer girl," I tell students as a photo of myself appears on the classroom projection screen.

In the photo, I am eight years old. My hand is on my hip, and I'm rocking a floppy hat and a T-shirt with horizontal stripes. My freckles are prominent, as is the contentment of my smile. I am a mixtape maker, an animal rescuer, and a notebook filler with aspirations of becoming an author.

"But becoming an author isn't how life played out—at least not for the first several decades of my life," I explain.

When it came time to choose my life course at the end of high school, I chose the sure thing. I settled for *what I thought* people wanted me to do and *what I thought* I could do without failing. It wasn't that I didn't want to be a teacher—I did. But leaving behind my dream of becoming an author also meant abandoning the dreamer girl inside. As I dedicated my time, focus, and energy

21

to teaching special education students, my writing fell by the way-side, and somewhere in the demands of everyday life, a part of my soul went missing.

Despite an ever-present feeling of unease, I carried on, forcing a bright smile so no one—not even I—could see the pain that was running deep in my being.

As the years passed, my uneasiness grew heavier, and my collection of masks grew larger as I expanded my masquerading skills into people pleasing and a never-ending quest for external validation. I became an expert at pretending to be happy when, secretly, I felt like I was dying inside. I made decisions about my life based on what I thought the world wanted from me without reflecting on my innermost desires. For nearly twenty years into adulthood, that is how I existed, until the pain of living an inau-thentic life could not be silenced anymore.

My children, Natalie and Avery, were around ages seven and four when the pain caused by my lack of self-love and self-care began manifesting in high-pitched, manic eruptions of tears fueled by despair. Caring for two small children in a new city while my husband, Scott, traveled for work; renewing my teaching certifica-tion; and managing excessive commitments and distractions put me in a perpetual state of stress. I felt overwhelmed, inadequate, and ashamed, and I often dreamed of running away from it all. In hind-sight, I understand how the emptiness of living an inauthentic life, layer after layer, year after year, is what made me long to escape.

One night, in a fleeting moment of panic, I made it all the way out to the car in my pajamas. I shivered against the cold leather seats. The sensation of pressing my bare foot against the gas pedal triggered a long-lost memory from my childhood. Though the adult in me was gripping the steering wheel and poised for escape, the little girl in me was swaying back and forth on the tire swing in my front yard back in Iowa, barefoot . . . carefree . . . and most notably, hope-filled.

While I hadn't listened to it in years, the faint voice of the dreamer girl in me was too familiar to ignore.

Remember me? she whispered into the heavy, hopeless silence of what had been, just moments ago, my getaway car.

"Yes," I said. "I remember you."

I leaned my head back and allowed the memories of that little girl in. I could almost feel the warm sensation of the sun on my face, reflecting on all of the things that made her me, when I was flooded with the notion that I was divinely designed for a unique purpose.

In an instant and for the first time in decades, I knew exactly what I needed to do *for me*. I needed to recover my voice, the one that spoke truth from the depths of my soul. I needed to live out my life in words and actions that aligned with who I'd been born to be—a writer.

I was not supposed to escape my current reality, but rather reflect and redefine it in my truest voice. And by doing so, I would save my life, as well as the lives of the two little girls I'd left standing in the kitchen with tear-streaked faces. What I didn't know in that moment—but would learn after years of trial and error—was that having a parent who lived by her truth would also increase my children's chances of living their own authentic lives rather than constantly measuring themselves by the standards or expectations of other people—including me!

The day after my attempted escape, I bought a spiral-bound notebook. Ironically, it was just like the one I had used decades ago in my college poetry class. About midway through the semester of that poetry class, students were required to turn in their notebooks for review. In mine, the professor wrote, "You have a powerful voice, Rachel."

I vividly remember the distinction my professor made between simply going through the motions of completing the writing exercises and actually using them as a means of growth, healing, and enlightenment. She taught me that in order to truly gain something meaningful from the writing prompts she'd given us, we had to be honest with ourselves. So that is what I began to do: I practiced being honest with myself.

What hadn't dawned on me as a sophomore in college hit me all those years later when I most needed a passageway back to my truest self: *It is only when I speak my greatest fears, admit my most difficult truths, proclaim my greatest longings, and shed light on my darkest thoughts that I feel heard, truly alive, and at peace.*

Each morning before the sun came up, I began writing in my crisp, new notebook. At night after my children went to bed, I'd write again—releasing trapped emotions, letting go of repressed memories, and liberating shameful thoughts with every line. Through those pages, my manic outbursts diminished, and my truest voice surfaced. Through those pages, I felt validated by something far greater than worldly approval; I felt guided by the One who could offer me true peace and fulfillment.

I was never more certain that I was doing exactly what I was made to do. Chronicling my truths reunited me with the dreamer girl inside and empowered me to become the author I felt called to be. As an unexpected bonus, this process also allowed me to clearly see each of my children and take notice of the messages I was sending them that either sabotaged or supported their truest selves. Although my path to accepting my children "just as they are" was far from perfect and often painful, I am thankful for the awareness I now have. Because this truth is grounded in the realization of my own diminished dreams, it never fails to open a passageway for me to reach them.

Standing in the classroom one day, at the end of another career day talk, looking through the notes written on index cards, it was evident that my honest confessions and vulnerability resonated with the students. An overwhelming number of young people shared the stress and pain of feeling unseen, unheard, and unaccepted for who they are. So many of their index cards gave me a glimpse into the various masks kids today are wearing— masks that I know all too well will only grow heavier as they continue down an unauthentic path.

- *My mom is really great and loving towards me and same with my dad, but they don't know what my dream is, and they have already taken it away from me—they just don't know it.*
- *I put on a smile. People think I'm the happiest person in the world. I act as normal as possible. I break down only when I'm at home alone.*
- *I fear I am unlovable, and this fear dictates my life.*
- *Mom and Dad, I want you to see the amount of pain and stress I deal with all the time.*
- *Kids need to talk to people they trust, and they should be able to talk to their parents without their parents judging them or hating them for what they do.*
- *I wish my parents understood that I am not an athlete.*
- *I wish my parents knew what was going on now, and how things aren't the same now as they were twenty-five years ago.*

The teen years have always been an awkward period in which young people attempt to find their own identities. But the world we live in today makes this life stage considerably more challenging—not only for our young people, but also for the adults whose job it is to help them navigate their way safely and securely into purposeful lives.

In our media-saturated, highly competitive, fast-paced culture, young people feel extreme pressure to conform to unrealistic and conflicting expectations. This constant pressure to be someone they're not in order to gain approval comes from all directions—school, peers, media, and home. As evidenced by the stacks of index cards I've collected over the past three years, teens feel it's necessary to project an enhanced or filtered version of themselves to the world in hopes of social acceptance, even if that image doesn't truly align with their values, interests, or strengths. The practice of curating an inauthentic self can be damaging and stressful for anyone, but especially to young people who are trying to establish their core identity and find their purpose.

We cannot control all the conflicting messages our kids receive, but we *can* control the messages they receive from us. Leading and raising kids these days requires more than modeling, more than imparting knowledge. It requires a whole new kind of self-awareness and communication. We must pay very careful attention to the messages we send our kids. Their actions or words might imply they no longer care about what adults think, but I have stacks and stacks of notecards telling me just the opposite. Truth be told, if we meet them where they are, without judgment, we have the opportunity to impart messages of acceptance to counter the insecurity that fuels many of the challenges young people face today, and we can thereby have a vital impact on young lives.

One of the most empowering gifts we can give kids is the permission and space to show up bravely exactly as they are, even if they don't think "who they are" is what the world wants to see. We can communicate this permission and create conditions for authenticity to thrive in at least three key ways:

- By being honest with ourselves about who we are, removing our masks, and tending to the places in ourselves where growth and healing are needed.
- By leaning in when our kids show us who they are and not making their choices and emotions about us.
- By being aware of the confining boxes and damaging labels society places on young people, and either rejecting them or reframing them as strengths.

In the pages ahead, we'll explore how to achieve these conditions by extending acceptance in three strategic ways: through *Refuge*, *Reframing*, and *Respect*.

When we support our young people to develop their most authentic selves, they are each better equipped to build a meaningful life from which they don't feel compelled to escape, numb out, hide, or merely endure. When we offer them our unconditional love, acceptance, and support, they can better connect to their dreamer within—that bare-footed, hope-filled part of themselves that feels alive, content, and filled with confidence that they have a unique role in this world. With us by their sides, our kids can develop the courage to live proudly in their own skin, no mask necessary.

ACCEPTANCE THROUGH REFUGE

Growing up, my refuge was my home. After my daily check-in with my dad at his office, I chose to walk three miles home rather than wait until his six o'clock quitting time. Home was where I most wanted to be.

Peace always washed over me as I closed the door of my house behind me. I actually leaned against it for a moment and exhaled with relief. The world couldn't touch me now. All day at school, I held my breath, sucked in my stomach, made sure to laugh when appropriate and not too loudly, and hid the extra-sensitive parts of myself that made me feel different. It was exhausting work.

At home, I could be myself; I could breathe. My parents loved my sister and me just as we were, and that unconditional acceptance permeated the walls of our home.

That's why, years later, it didn't surprise me that my mom was the first to notice my seven-year-old daughter's dimming light. Avery had always been the one to light up the world with her smile. The change in her temperament had been evident to me, too, but I'd blamed it on a recent move from our tightly knit community to a large, metropolitan area. For months, I refused to look at myself as the source of Avery's pain. After all, I'd stopped telling her to hurry all the time. I'd corralled my exasperated breaths and tapered the impatience in my voice. I'd deemed her a "Noticer" who paid attention to the most important details of life and people.

Avery did things differently than me—than most—but I'd stopped fighting it. Instead, I tolerated it. But had I accepted it? Accepted her? *No.* It was becoming impossible to deny the look of concern on her face as we left the house for school each morning, as if she was wondering whether or not she was enough for the world.

My mom's comment about Avery's dimming light told me I had yet more work to do. Reflecting on the way I reconnected with my passion for writing, I thought about the things that make Avery's heart dance. It hit me: music. Avery had picked up a ukulele at age three and never stopped strumming it. Music was her medium, and she needed a space to be enveloped in it.

I rolled up my sleeves and set to work on a small room at the front of our new house that had been designated a quiet reading room. I redesignated it "Avery's music room." It was one of the few rooms painted a colorful hue—a soft, calming blue like the summer sky. It would be a place of refuge for my songbird.

Avery excitedly set up her guitar, ukulele, music stand, and microphone. She added notebooks and pencils for music writing, and like clockwork each evening, she'd go to the music room and play.

Yes, she was strumming and singing, but to me, it sounded like breathing.

It was *her* sigh of relief against the front door.

"What did you write?" I'd ask, joining her after a few minutes. As she showed me the songs she'd written, I couldn't help but notice two common themes repeating: being okay just as you are, and God's unfailing love. Avery would sing to me, and I would marvel. It wasn't long before she expressed a desire to play for people outside the music room.

"All right," I said. "Let's start thinking about where you could do that."

A few days later, while we were on a walk, Avery articulated the hardest thing about moving to a new place. Expressing how much she missed our old neighborhood where everyone knew her name and the retirement home we'd visit with friends from church, she said something I'll never forget: "I just want to be known."

An invitation to a music therapy session at a local nursing home opened the door for her to have a place to be known—and more importantly, by a person. As Avery played along with the music therapist, one of the residents—I'll call her Annie—seemed particularly happy and engaged in their music. We quickly learned that Annie loved music above all else. Her favorite musician was Elvis. When we heard Annie hadn't had a visitor in many years, Avery suggested we adopt her. Then, when we got home, Avery went right to her music room and began working on learning "Fools Rush In."

During our nursing home visits, Avery was extremely patient with Annie, pointing out birds and butterflies in the garden, asking thoughtful questions, and nodding in understanding to nonsensical responses. Sometimes, when they painted, Annie's arm got tired and she'd hand the paintbrush to Avery. Avery would finish Annie's picture, no words needed.

Some days, Avery would wake up and say, "I think we need to see Annie today." Often her suggestion would fall on a day that was already quite full, making a long trek to the retirement home the last thing I wanted to do. But I usually obliged, knowing that Avery was listening to her heart and that its priorities were far more urgent than anything on a to-do list. With that frame of mind, I was able to see the drive not as a hassle, but as an opportunity to connect.

One day, as we drove to the retirement center, I said, "You are a delight, Avery."

"I am?" she asked, looking shocked.

"Yes," I said, immediately feeling sad that I'd never mentioned it before. "You are delight-*ful*, and I love being with you."

As Avery smiled for the rest of the drive, I promised myself I'd never assume my children knew they were a marvel to me.

Sometimes we'd arrive at the nursing home to find Annie despondent or agitated. But not once did Avery suggest we leave or cut our visit short. She'd push Annie's wheelchair outside, where she loved to sit by the fountain. Avery would sit with her and sing to her, as if to say, *It's okay. I know you aren't yourself today.*

For months, we continued to visit the nursing home, never knowing the state of mind Annie would be in when we arrived. On one particularly hard day, Annie's deterioration was evident; she appeared to be a shell of her former self. We couldn't see a single trace of the vibrant Annie we'd met during that initial music therapy session.

When we first arrived, Annie was angry, but then she began to sob uncontrollably. That's when Avery bent down, got close to Annie's face, and began to sing softly. When she did, I heard the unmistakable sound of an exhale. It was as if Annie had been holding her breath and the music allowed her to feel at home again.

In my mind's eye, I could see the door to my house . . . the one I'd lean against when I got home . . . the one I felt safe standing behind because it was where I was loved "as is."

With Avery, Annie was home. Avery gave her a refuge.

Avery's music communicated safety and acceptance to Annie. Regardless of the actual song lyrics, Avery's verses for Annie conveyed reassurance:

You are not yourself right now, but I accept you.
You are difficult to handle, but I accept you.
You are different, but I accept you.

A few months after that powerful moment with Annie, I was invited to attend an award ceremony at Avery's school. She was being recognized for the essay she'd entered in the county-wide Honoring Our Heroes writing program. Students were asked to recognize someone who had made a personal impact on their life—Avery had chosen me. Her reasoning, summed up in the last line of her essay, brought great confirmation to my heart: "My mom is my hero because she accepts me for who I am, and she inspires acceptance to spread in the world through her writing."

To think, I'd nearly settled for giving Avery *tolerance*, the bare minimum of what she needed in order to get by in the world.

But her dimming light was a warning sign that tolerance was not enough.

So I gave her *acceptance*—a place to breathe, to be herself, to cultivate her gifts.

As a result, she was able to give acceptance to someone else— someone who just happened to be at the end of her life.

Is there any greater way to *end* a life than with acceptance?

Is there any greater way to *begin* a life than with acceptance?

I don't think so.

I used to think listening was the most important gift adults could give to build up their kids. Now, given the stressors and lack of restorative spaces in the twenty-first century, I think acceptance is equally vital. In fact, listening and acceptance actually go hand in hand.

Be the one who doesn't try to change them.

Be the one who detects all that is good in them.

Be the one who identifies their unique contributions to the world and encourages them.

Be the one who delights in them and tells them so.

Of all the offerings you can give your kids today, give acceptance. Be the place where they are known, seen, heard, and celebrated. Over time, that unconditional acceptance will serve as inner armor, protecting their sense of self when the world tries to negate it.

Who knows? Someday you might be called a hero—but not the kind you see on the news for triumphant acts of bravery. I'm talking about the hero who quietly, behind the scenes, on a day-to-day basis listens and loves without condition, without restraint, without timetable, and without expectation.

You might not have started out a hero.

I certainly didn't.

But every time a special young lady picks up her instrument, I am reminded that it's never too late to do what I wish I would've done yesterday.

It's the most beautiful song my soul has ever heard.

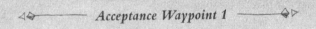

Acceptance Waypoint 1

STAND ASIDE

When parents approach me at speaking events, I often recognize a common emotion: *fear*. Fear of the distance that has come between themselves and their kids, fear of the damaging influences that are beyond their control, fear of being unprepared to help their kids navigate a world so different from the one in which they themselves grew up. One parent I spoke to described how terrifying it was to find her daughter bleeding from self-inflicted scratches, and worse, having to admit to herself that until she'd discovered her child's behavior, she'd known nothing of her pain.

"What can I do?" the mother asked in desperation.

Hugging the woman tightly, I asked the first question that came to my mind: "Does your daughter have a place away from the pressures, the noise, and the judgment of the world to do something she loves to do? Does she have a refuge?"

The woman shook her head and said, "Not really." I've since learned her daughter is receiving therapy and finding peace riding horses and painting. Her mother reported that the light is slowly coming back into her child's eyes.

I believe in the power of a refuge, which can come in many forms, such as soul-building mentors, peaceful places, stress-relieving activities, or passions. The problem is, sometimes we actually stand in our kids' way of having these people, places, and activities.

I stood in my daughter's way when I critiqued her guitar practice.

I stood in my daughter's way when I pushed her toward certain activities and away from others.

I stood in her way when I limited the time she spent with soul-building influencers because I didn't want to burden other people.

I stood in my daughter's way when I set standards for the activities that brought her joy.

But then I recognized what all that standing in the way really was—I was attempting to protect myself, not her, and I was blocking the light from reaching my daughter's eyes.

Now, I try to stand for creating a refuge so kids can be who they are. I stand for ensuring that the young people in my life have a place where they can breathe freely and explore, but this requires some effort and some uncomfortable truths.

- Sometimes we may not be able to give our children everything they need to thrive, but maybe someone else can. We need to be willing to ask for help and allow other people to teach, guide, and equip our kids.
- Taking them to their places of refuge might require a willingness to be inconvenienced.
- Their passion might not be what we had hoped or planned for their lives.
- There might be gaps of uncertainty between activities or interests. We need to trust that those gaps will be filled in time and in unexpected ways if we remain open to possibilities outside our control.
- When they say someone makes them feel uncomfortable or inferior, we will need to listen carefully.

When the human spirit can't breathe, it begins to suffocate. When the human spirit can't shine, it begins to dim. Spending time in a place or with a person of refuge builds inner armor for the pitfalls, pressures, and pains of life so that no matter what the world says about them, our kids will see it as an opinion and not their truth, their path, or their purpose. Now, more than ever, kids need a refuge.

Let's step aside, or better yet, lead them to find such a refuge rather than stand in their way.

ACCEPTANCE THROUGH REFRAMING

Interestingly, sometime after I'd begun writing again, many of Natalie's concerning behaviors began to disappear. She stopped picking her lip until it bled. She stopped second-guessing herself when she made a decision. She stopped berating herself when she made a mistake. As I practiced my determination to recover *my* truest voice and discover *my* most authentic self, I'd adopted a new loving and compassionate way of talking to myself, and it hadn't gone unnoticed by my daughter. As I began showing up without a mask—flawed, but full of hope—Natalie did, too.

I'm not sure I would have connected the dots between my healing and Natalie's blossoming had it not been for a message I received from my parents. I'd sent them a picture of Natalie working in her garden one morning—a garden she'd dug herself, right in the middle of the backyard.

My parents' response was this:

> Thanks for this precious picture of our beautiful grand-daughter. Over the last two years, we have seen a tremendous change in her. We no longer see a scared look in her eyes; she is less fearful about you being upset or impatient with her. She is much happier and more relaxed. She is thriving and growing into a content, creative, and nurturing person. We know for a fact that the changes we see in her coincide with the changes we have also seen in you.

My parents' hopeful observation encouraged me to continue being true to who I was, even at the risk of rejection, so that my children could be confident in who they were, too. It wasn't easy at first to let go of long-held, damaging beliefs and instead lean into who my daughter truly was. In fact, one of the first times Natalie showed me who she was, all I could think about was how her deepest longing would affect me.

Natalie asked if she could hold a summer camp in our home for several neighborhood children. I immediately said no. My reasons: *It will make a mess. You'll start projects and never finish them. I'll have to do all the work.* Those reasons were all assumptions based on my own insecurities, fears, and personal agenda. But the following summer, when Natalie asked again, I was able to see that the request was about her, not about me, and that letting her follow her desire could shape her self-identity. Natalie honored the commitment she made to do all the lesson planning, all the supply purchasing, and all the teaching herself. And each afternoon, young friends from the neighborhood showed up at our door, ready to be taught by their beloved teacher, Miss Natalie.

Between the backyard garden and the summer camp, I began to see the emergence of Natalie's inherent gifts and spirited personality. Oftentimes, Natalie's fearlessness made me uncomfortable. But instead of clenching at control, I released and trusted the path of a child whose zest for life could not be contained.

Natalie was a brave path-forger, willing to venture into unfamiliar territories in order to better herself and others. She was a curious learner, cultivating the art of discovering answers to her questions. She was a seed planter, taking small glimmers of hope and nurturing them into real possibilities.

For eight consecutive years (minus the summer our family moved to a new state), Natalie held summer camp in our home for the neighbor kids. I found it interesting that she never repeated the same theme. The vivacious learner in her chose camp topics based on her interests at the time, related to topics she wanted to know more about. Whether it was Super Science, Undercover Spy, Art, Fashionista, Olympics, or Pet Camp, Natalie thoroughly enjoyed the planning and research process that went into producing camp each year. There was always something special about the way she relayed her findings that made her students feel as though she was widening her horizons alongside them as they learned.

Then, just as fourteen-year-old Natalie began planning a World Traveler camp, she received a letter from the host organization that had originally sparked her interest in Africa through the sponsorship of a child named Priscilla. For seven years, Natalie and Priscilla had faithfully corresponded with each other, sharing sacred details of their lives. Natalie dreamt of the day she would travel to Ghana to meet her friend. But upon opening this particular letter from the organization, Natalie's hopes were dashed. Without warning, Natalie was informed that Priscilla was no longer part of the program, and that there would be no more correspondence between them.

My daughter, who typically keeps her emotions in check, was devastated.

"I don't understand," Natalie said quietly. "I didn't get to say goodbye. Priscilla was my friend."

I wondered how this abrupt ending would impact Natalie's travel goals. But rather than deter her from her original dream of traveling to Africa, this unexpected heartbreak seemed to fuel it.

"I still want to go there," Natalie said with fierce determination the following day.

In that moment, I saw her truth clearer than I ever had before; she was a Wanderer forging new paths and would go to Africa, one way or another, with or without me.

I nervously released a silent prayer heavenward: *If she goes, let me go alongside her.*

As the months passed, I began voicing my prayer aloud while conversing with people in my professional and personal life about the possibility. This public admission led to a long conversation with the cofounder of African Road, a nonprofit organization that partners with local East African ChangeMakers to lift communities out of poverty through collaborative project development and strategic funding.

"African Road Learning Trips are not *doing* trips, they are *being* trips," the cofounder, Kelly, explained to me over the phone. "Travelers are invited into the living rooms of ChangeMakers, friends of African Road. I love introducing friends to friends and seeing what can become possible through friendship. Instead of asking you to come and fix, mend, or build, we ask you to arrive open in heart and mind and ready to learn from these wise, grass-roots leaders in East Africa. They are the experts, and we go to be present. We put our agenda and expectations aside and come with a willingness to be open and attentive. We keep in mind that things won't always go as planned, and we must adapt and flex. In Swahili, the words '*polepole*' [polay-polay] mean *go slowly, slowly*. And this is what we believe: good things come by going slowly and being present. It's the coming alongside that matters."

The hairs on my arms stood up. The way of African Road sounded much like the way I had learned to love my daughter into who she was becoming.

Holding my breath, I asked, "Could my fourteen-year-old daughter apply for the Learning Trip?"

"If she is with you," Kelly replied.

It sounded a lot like an answer to my prayer.

When I told Natalie about the conversation, her reaction provided further confirmation. Blinking back tears, she said, "Really? You would do this with me?"

Because I'd spent the previous eight years of her life no longer hiding who I was, Natalie knew me. She knew her directionally-challenged, anxiety-prone mother prefers familiar territories and best-laid plans. She knew that going abroad would be far out of my comfort zone, but that I was listening to my intuitive voice, God's urging, which said, *Go. In time, you will understand why.*

The trip began to be a blessing long before it was a reality. Natalie was so eager to talk about it that she asked if we could start hiking on Sunday afternoons to discuss it. As she was beginning to enter the typical distancing stage teens often go through and spending more time with her peers, our Sunday afternoon walks were a true gift.

During the four-mile loop, Natalie would talk about East Africa. In the same manner that she had prepared for her summer camps, she was immersing herself in all things East Africa—

learning the language, its history, its customs, its adversities, and its triumphs.

In the spring, the topic of discussion during our hikes took a marked turn, and I was never more thankful for this sacred connection time. Africa was only the subject during the initial minutes, then the conversation shifted to end-of-the-year testing, grades, and course scheduling for Natalie's upcoming high school year.

One particular conversation stands out. My strong, nerves-of-steel daughter was unusually sensitive that day. As we walked the trail, she expressed frustration with her wandering brain. Focusing in school has always been a challenge for her, but at that particular time, her struggles were heightened by more complex content and memorization requirements. Despite her support systems and having sought medical advice, she felt daunted by school, and uncertainty loomed. Coping mechanisms that had worked for her in the past were no longer working. All at once, Natalie felt her future was in question.

"What if I can't stay on track in high school? What will become of me?" she asked, her voice heavy with pain.

I touched my daughter's arm to slow her down. We stopped there on the path we'd walked together for many months. As I looked into her brown eyes, I saw the little gardener and the young teacher who could now offer proof of her strengths in her time of weakness.

"Natalie, you are a Wanderer," I said aloud for the first time.

I went on to explain how her way of *being* creates challenges in certain settings and situations. That the educational system might lead her to believe that being a Wanderer is a problem, and that her path is not the "right" path. But then I encouraged her to look at her past.

"Natalie, you've already spent much of your young life forging the way," I reminded her. "You seek to gain understanding of places and people far from home and teach others what you learn. You've done this year after year with much success—the kind of success that has already made a lasting impact and will leave a loving legacy."

I wanted her to understand that taking her own path is not just okay, but imperative for her personal well-being. "Your path might look different than the track the school pushes you toward, but that is a good thing!" I said. "Your Wanderer ways have served you well and will continue to serve you well for the rest of your life. And I'm honored to come alongside you on *your* path."

The sigh Natalie released in that moment indicated that my reframing of her perceived weakness into a positive trait, along with the assurance of my support and belief in her, was exactly what she needed.

Despite the conflicting messages she was receiving from society, Natalie believed what I was saying about her was true because *I knew her*, and she knew me.

Many months later, I learned that was the day Natalie started a Wanderer journal. She began collecting quotes that spoke to her Wanderer heart. There must have been fifty inspiring quotes about leaving one's comfort zone in order to find purpose, cultivate inner peace, and fully experience life.

Although many of the quotes focused on travel, the central theme was overcoming fear and seemed to apply perfectly to the new territories Natalie was navigating in school, peer relationships, and physical changes. Her journal reminded her of who she was and who she was divinely designed to be, even when the world told her otherwise.

Validating Natalie's unique gifts stoked a flame in her soul, which was all she needed to feel assured that her purpose and path were not only warranted but intended.

It is painful to acknowledge that I nearly sabotaged Natalie's ability to navigate life as her true, authentic self, but that is when I remind myself that *today matters more than yesterday*. And today, I look to Natalie and to the other brave Wanderers of the world who remind us not to be paralyzed by fear or uncertainty, but instead to forge ahead.

To move.
Go beyond the horizon.
Step outside our comfort zones.
Plant a seed.
Nurture our gifts and the gifts of others.

It is not our job to decide if these gifts, interests, and inclinations are good or bad, but to trust that they are divinely designed with a purpose.

Perhaps if we step back, we can see the bigger picture for the ones we love and an expanded view of our own personal journey toward wholeness.

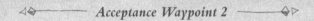

◁◈——— *Acceptance Waypoint 2* ———◈▷

THE GOOD NEWS

I was warned about age thirteen, and I must admit, the warnings created anxiety and negative expectations. I realized I was bracing myself for the horrendous things I'd read and heard about. Perhaps you've heard the same stereotypes. It's hard not to. Guess who else hears them? Thirteen-year-olds. I got a clear picture of how fully my thirteen-year-old daughter comprehended the damage of this stereotype when Natalie showed me a poem she wrote for a creative writing class.

Just Because

Just because I'm a teenager
I am not irresponsible
I don't break every single rule
It doesn't mean I am lazy and unorganized.

Just because I'm a teenager
It doesn't mean I'm moody and rude
It doesn't mean I only think about myself
And it doesn't mean I'm addicted to my phone.

Just because I'm a teenager
It doesn't mean I'm constantly worried about my appearance
It doesn't mean I don't understand complex subjects
Or that I don't have real goals and aspirations.
Because I'm a teenager—get to know me for who I am, not how
I'm labeled.

When I read Natalie's poem, I thought of several people I wanted to send it to.

I wanted to send it to the youth minister of a church we visited shortly after our move. While addressing the congregation, he made a joke about parents wanting to "ship off" their teens. Everyone laughed while my daughter shifted uncomfortably in her seat.

I wanted to send it to the grocery store clerk who looked at my happy child a few years ago and said, "Just you wait. Once she becomes a teenager, all that sweetness disappears."

I wanted to send it to the man who laughed and rudely interrupted his daughter when she spoke to me because, "Teenagers just like to hear themselves talk."

I wanted to send it to every person who routinely dismisses

the words, ideas, and opinions of teens because they think they are not valid, logical, or serious.

What some adults don't realize about such negative labels is that they stick, they influence, they harm, and they undermine. They can mean the difference between floundering and flourishing, between holding on or giving up—and not just for teens, but for the people who love them.

Parents of younger children often ask me if the teen years are as bad as they've heard. It brings me great joy to tell them of the many positive qualities I've witnessed as both a high school teacher and a mother of adolescents.

"I think teens are pretty amazing," I say, hoping my positive description might help debunk a label or two.

Labels that stereotype are damaging for many reasons, but perhaps the biggest one is that they cause us to deny the critical stage teens are in—a stage of growing into themselves, finding their way, and cultivating their strengths and gifts. It is a phase of life in which they most need us as allies—people who see the best in them, so that they are more likely to see it in themselves.

If things have been difficult with a young person you love, there are steps you can take to earn your role as an ally.

- Consider the negative stereotypes that may have influenced your feelings or made you feel unequipped, and let them go.
- Offer yourself a blank slate by looking at your beloved and remembering a favorite memory of him or her as a small child. That promise you saw in your child's eyes is still there, and your child needs you to see it now more than ever.
- Reframe negative labels into strengths:
  - "Too sensitive" can become "deep feeler."
  - "Unmotivated" can become "selective."

- "Overly anxious" can become "fierce protector."
- "Shy" can become "introspective."
- "Distracted" can become "noticer."
- Reframing allows you to essentially redesign negative labels through a positive vision. By looking at your child through a positive lens, you are in better position to be his light protector or her soul-builder.

The most vital thing to remember when young people are going through turbulent times is that their goodness and light have not disappeared—they just may have gotten squelched. By reframing thoughts and situations in a positive light, not only do you establish yourself as a supportive confidant, but you also model how to keep one's attitude strong and hopeful, even in the face of negative opinion or circumstances.

ACCEPTANCE THROUGH RESPECT

Natalie doesn't drink coffee, but she drinks from the same beloved coffee mug every morning. Her cup says, "A fun thing to do in the morning is NOT TALK TO ME."

I was with her when she bought it. I remember hearing her laugh out loud in that quaint, beachside gift shop. I remember how she took the mug from the shelf and began digging in her purse for money.

Now I find her in the kitchen, before the sun comes up, with tea or just plain old water in that cup. She has it positioned just so: message facing out, so no one forgets.

I could take offense, but that would be a waste of precious time. And time is already going too quickly—it takes my breath away. Plus, I was a teenager once. I actually remember clearing my throat one morning after years of listening to my parents' well-meaning dialogue and inquisitive questions. I was a freshman in high school.

"I don't like to talk in the morning," I bravely announced. "Can you *not* . . . talk to me?" I asked.

My parents looked a little surprised, but they were unfazed, unoffended, understanding.

"Okay," they said, turning to talk to one another. I can remember how delighted and empowered I felt as I ate my Raisin Bran in silence all the days that followed.

My preferred time to talk was nighttime. When I wanted to talk, I knew where to find my mom—in the living room, wearing her velvety, rose-colored robe with the zipper up the front, reading her mystery novel. When I'd come into the room, she'd look up and smile, flipping the book over as if to say, *Yes, I'd love nothing more than to talk with you, Rachel. Please, come in.*

I can remember the barrage of adolescent worries and complaints that poured from my mouth so quickly it was almost embarrassing. But Mom was unfazed and understanding. Sometimes, I wanted advice, but mostly I just wanted someone to listen when I was ready to talk—on my terms, and most certainly *not* in the morning.

It helps me as a parent to remember that important declaration of who I was and what felt comfortable to me, and how my parents honored and respected the boundary I'd drawn.

My teen doesn't need me as often as she once did. I can see how much she relishes her friend time and her alone time. Sometimes, when I offer up ideas or suggestions, they are quickly dismissed. My invitations are often declined. I come second to Google for medical questions, makeup tutorials, and tech help. There are times when my teen turns up the radio in the car and says, "I just want to hear this song. Let's be quiet." There are times when she pulls away.

I could take offense, but that would be a waste of precious time.

It would also create a barrier between us,
when all my daughter is doing is setting boundaries,
and boundaries are life giving and lifesaving.

Boundaries allow us to separate who we are, and what we think and feel, from the thoughts and feelings of others. Setting boundaries helps us protect ourselves; they are the deepest act of self-care there is.

So instead of being offended, I make myself available and approachable for the times I am the one she wants to come to, and for those sacred moments when the worries come tumbling out. In such moments, I am invited into her world that is evolving, growing, forming, strengthening, and becoming beautifully independent, colorful, fascinating, and promising.

Yes, my teenager's world has boundaries, just as it should.

And they will protect her in the days and months and years to come.

And they will come quickly, this I know for sure.

So I choose not to be offended.

Time is much too precious for that.

◁☙ ———— *Acceptance Waypoint 3* ———— ❖▷

SEVEN WAYS TO HELP KIDS FIND THEIR TRUEST VOICE

1. BE AVAILABLE

Consistently look up from the task at hand and into your loved one's eyes. Your gaze indicates you value their thoughts, no matter how trivial. This nonverbal sign of availability provides both a foundation and an invitation to more difficult conversations as they grow.

From time to time, ask yourself, *Do my non-verbal cues indicate that I am approachable and available when my kid needs to talk?* No matter how tired you are, no matter how busy you are, no matter how bad a day you had, you reap rich benefits when your actions demonstrate that love is never "off the clock." By mustering up a loving hello for the everyday conversations, you are more likely to be the one your kid seeks out in times of despair and challenge.

2. FOLLOW THE 80/20 RULE

Attentively listening to your children's dreams, needs, and questions results in the ability to know them intimately. When we feel known, we feel loved and understood in the most powerful way possible. Acclaimed child and adolescent psychotherapist Katie Hurley encourages parents to connect with their kids by following the 80/20 rule—80 percent listening, 20 percent talking. She says, "One thing young clients tell me over and over again: 'I just want my parents to listen.'"[1]

Although it is understandable to want to offer solutions and "fix" whatever is troubling our kids, doing so sends a message that they are not capable of handling things themselves. By listening, you become a sounding board to help kids be their own problem solvers, which becomes a lifelong gift.

---

1. Katie Hurley, LCSW. Facebook, February 28, 2019, https://www.facebook.com/katiehurleylcsw/photos/a.367620819915505/2825678914109671/?type=3&theater.

3. GIVE TIME AND SPACE

Maybe it takes time for your kids to put their thoughts into words. It's okay; you don't have to finish their sentences—the words will come. Maybe their opinion is completely nuts. It's okay; you don't have to agree. Maybe they remember something differently than you do. It's okay; you don't have to be "right." By giving them the time and space to share what's on their minds and in their hearts, you are strengthening their voices.

4. MODEL AUTHENTICITY

The next time you're hurting, resist the inclination to put on a brave face or to rationalize withdrawal because you don't want to trouble anyone or because other people have it worse than you. Instead, be honest. Saying, "I'm not okay," is often the first step to feeling better. Letting yourself cry, be angry, or be scared is often the first step to moving forward. And allowing yourself to *feel* is often the first step to healing. These are all healthy expressions to model for our kids. Our kids need to know that saying how we really feel to a trusted person is brave, healing, and helpful.

In our family, a comforting question to ask in the quiet of bedtime or in the sanctuary of the car is, "How are you *really* doing?" And then we just listen—listen without the need to fix, judge, or dismiss.

5. LET THEM SPEAK FOR THEMSELVES

From the time they were very young, I have encouraged my kids to speak to their coaches, waiters, teachers, and salespeople when they have something to say. I remember distinctly when this practice paid off. We were sitting at my child's fifth grade parent/teacher conference, and the teacher asked if we had any concerns. My daughter spoke up to say she loved helping her classmates, but there was one male student who made her feel very uncomfortable, and she would not be able to help him anymore.

By allowing kids to speak for themselves in routine situations, we are preparing them to use their voices in difficult situations that threaten their rights and safety as well as the rights and safety of others.

6. WATCH YOUR JUDGMENT

What judgments do you voice about your teen's classmates, teammates, friends, other parents, teachers, leaders, and favorite celebrities? When you express harsh judgments about other people's choices and the way they live their lives, you are leading your kids to believe you will also make judgments about them. In an effort to shield themselves from your disapproval, your kids may begin to hold back information about themselves, limiting your chance of ever truly knowing them.

7. CONSISTENTLY OFFER ACCEPTANCE

Do your kids know that they do not need to do anything, be anything, or change anything to be loved by you? Instead of assuming they know, make it a point to frequently say, "I love you just as you are. Exactly as you are. I love you because you are you."

Feeling known and accepted by the people in your home not only makes for a better day, but it also makes for a better future.

LIVE LOVE NOW REFLECTION: THE PAUSE

I Am

Natalie Stafford

I am optimistic and kind.
I wonder where I'll be in twenty years.

I hear my pets talking to me.
I see a world full of good people.
I want to have a job that I love.
I am optimistic and kind.

I pretend that I am a seashell floating on the ocean floor.
I feel joy when I see a rainbow.
I touch a twinkling star.
I worry about the environment.
I cry when I watch sad news stories.

I understand there is a lot of bad in the world.
I say be unique and be yourself.
I dream about graduating college.
I try to be positive.
I hope to find goodness in everything.
I am optimistic and kind.

When I read this poem for the first time, it woke me up.
With painful clarity, I realized I needed to stop . . .
Stop focusing on fixing the shortcomings in my child, and start nurturing the strengths.
Stop predicting what she's going to make of herself, and start celebrating who she already is.

I keep her poem handy and read it often.
It reminds me to build her up . . .

By observing:

What makes her fearful?
What words make her smile?
What is she passionate about?
What breaks her heart?

By asking:

What are your dreams?
What do you wish the world understood about you?
If you could go anywhere, where would you go?
What frustrates you the most about school? About life?
What problem do you want to solve in the world?

By listening:

To her passionate complaints.
To her mature insights.
To her real pain.
To her deep breathing when she's catching up on sleep.

I'll never forget walking into her bedroom, her poem fresh on my mind.

I saw: Dirty bowls on the surfaces, clean clothes on the floor.
Pause.
I noticed: She'd laid two dresses on the bed.

"One of my classmates can't really afford a dress for the end-of-the-year dance," she said. "I thought she might like to wear one of mine."

Pause.

Blink back tears.

"I really think she'll like this one," she said, holding it up.

And then she twirled so that the dress lifted . . . right along with my heart.

She is . . .

More than her grades, her dirty dishes, and her forgetfulness.

She is ideas.

She is heart.

She is optimistic and kind.

I'm starting to see . . .

The pauses are just as important as the guidance, and perhaps more important than the words.

They make space to observe, to ask, to listen, and to remember.

She is, she *already* is . . .

Someone extraordinary.

Because of her, a friend has something beautiful to wear to the last dance of her middle-school career.

And that dress has the potential to twirl and to lift hearts right along with it.

That is who she is, and that is more than enough.

REFLECTION QUESTIONS

1. In what ways do you feel in tune or out of tune with your intuitive/truest voice? How have you let it guide you recently? What, if anything, interferes with your ability to hear or trust your truest voice?

2. In what ways recently have you allowed the young person in your life to fully express what he or she is feeling or thinking? In what ways have you suppressed his or her truest thoughts and emotions?

3. If the young person in your life was asked to list people who allow him or her to be authentic, do you think you would be on the list? Why or why not?

4. Think of three people you would describe as living authentically. What traits do they possess? Which of those traits would you like to cultivate? Write a daily intention that helps you take one small step toward living more freely as yourself.

5. How might a more authentic, accepting version of you benefit the young person in your life?

CHAPTER 2

REJECTED

*True belonging doesn't require you to change who you
are; it requires you to be who you are.*

—Brené Brown, *Braving the Wilderness*

During my early twenties, I remember being overly concerned
about my then-boyfriend's appearance and image. Now that I
understand I was adding layers to my mask of inauthenticity back
then, it makes sense that I forced them on him, too. I'd kindly
(and often not so kindly) instruct my boyfriend about what to
wear, how to eat healthy, and how often to exercise. Despite his
interests and strengths, I pushed him toward jobs that offered
status and prestige. I noticed the look of defeat in his eyes when
I offered up my "helpful suggestions," but nevertheless, I kept
saying them. After all, I wanted him to make a good impression.

This is for him, I told myself.

But was it? Or, subconsciously, was it all about me?

Beneath the critiques of his appearance and social status was
my fear—fear that *I* wasn't good enough, so I had to "prove" my
worth by associating with successful and attractive people.

It came as no surprise that I continued this critical behavior in my marriage and in my parenting. In fact, I took an excessive and unhealthy interest in my family members' "good impressions" in the areas of performance (sports, music, academics) and physical appearance. My critiques typically fell on a continuum from mildly constructive to downright destructive, depending how vulnerable I felt at the time.

"I just want *you* to make a good impression," I'd say.

It was for them, I'd tell myself. There it was again—my "good" intention.

Yet how could I explain the pain in their eyes—the pain I was seemingly willing to ignore in order to satisfy the ideal in my own head?

As with my former boyfriend, criticism of my family members originated with the belief that I needed to hide certain parts of myself in order to be loved and accepted.

This truth is not pretty, but it's healing—and it's life-changing.

I remember the day I came face-to-face with this painful truth. I'd been getting ready to attend a social gathering in our community. On the floor of my bathroom lay an array of discarded outfits. I hated the way I looked in all of them. Rage and insecurity bubbled up inside me as I finally settled on something dark and baggy. With my mouth set in a thin, hard line, I opened my daughter's bedroom door to see if she looked acceptable.

I found six-year-old Avery standing in front of the mirror. My eyes immediately zeroed in on the too-snug waistband of her favorite shorts. Flesh spilled over, clinging tightly to her flowered shirt. I lifted my eyes to the mismatched headband and messy knot of hair sprouting in more directions than weeds in a garden.

As I opened my mouth to remind Avery we needed to make our best impression, I caught a glimpse of her face in the mirror.

The expression reflecting back at her was quite different than mine; it was one of pure joy. Pure contentment. Pure peace—all at the sight of her six-year-old self.

Then she twirled in front of the mirror—actually twirled. Upon her second rotation, she saw me at the door, wiping tears from my eyes. She gave me a glorious smile—a smile that said, *I feel beautiful, Mama.*

And that's when I heard the protective, healing voice of my dreamer girl whisper, "Let her be."

Let her be.

For the first time in decades, I recognized my critiques for what they were: rejection. And in them, I heard the damaging message I was imprinting on my child's soul: *You are not enough. You will be rejected if you come as you are.*

I'd always justified my behavior by telling myself I was helping her fit in. In reality, I was planting seeds of self-doubt that would only cause her to believe she didn't belong. If I kept up my messages of judgment, they would eventually become Avery's inner voice, causing her to hold back her God-given gifts from the world.

Is this the life you want for your child? I asked myself.

Suddenly, it occurred to me that unlike Avery's blue eyes and freckles, which she inherited from me, she did not have to inherit my fear of rejection. Right then and there, I knew I had the power to decide *not* to pass my insecurity on to her.

Why would I want her to stand in front of the mirror for the rest of her life seeing *too much* and *not enough* when she could see *just right?*

Why would I want her to believe happiness could only be found in college acceptance letters and social media Likes when she could find happiness from within?

Why would I want her to navigate life hoping to be accepted by the "in" group when she could feel completely and lovingly supported by those who know and love her best?

Why would I want her to waste precious time wondering and worrying what other people think of her when *she* herself could be lovingly at peace with *who she is?*

It was then that I experienced a very necessary epiphany; one that led me toward healing and promise: *It is not my job to evaluate myself or my child. My job is to show up as I am—bravely, boldly, flawed, and full of hope—to share my gifts with the world. And in doing so, I provide an example that will encourage my child to connect with others as her most authentic self.*

I got out a spiral notebook, just as eight-year-old Rachel would have, and I wrote:

I release myself from being judge and jury. This means I do not decide I'm bad or good, worthy or unworthy, enough or not enough. This means I do not judge my feelings. Instead, I acknowledge them, sit with them, or voice them. It might sound like this:

> *Yes, I am scared, but I am still showing up.*
> *Yes, I feel less-than, but I am not letting it stop me.*
> *Yes, I'm anxious, but the unknowing is always the hardest part.*
> *Yes, I fear they won't like me, but we don't click with*
>   *everyone, and that is okay.*

Shifting from the role of evaluator to Truth-teller took considerable time, patience, and grace. I was able to find the motivation I needed to let my children "be" by envisioning the emotional well-being of their future selves. I did not want them to develop an identity of rejection that would make life even harder. I did not want them to make life choices based on approval rather than on staying true to their values, strengths, and dreams. Above all, I did not want my kids to live in fear of rejection, but instead feel empowered to connect with others on a foundation of truth, courage, and love.

I've had the opportunity to speak with young people about my journey to become a Truth-teller, and in doing so, I have received a great deal of feedback. The priceless comments I've compiled by way of what I now call my "Index Card Exercise" demonstrate how much today's kids yearn for true connection and unconditional acceptance from adults and each other.

- *I have not told my parents who I really am. Knowing them, they would not support it. I don't want to be hated or kicked out of the house because of who I am. Only the friends I know I can really trust know who I am, but my parents don't because I am scared of losing their love.*
- *I want my parents to understand it's not about the appearance of people—it's what's inside them.*
- *Love everybody no matter what skin color. Love everybody, and do not be mean to anybody.*
- *Adults need to hear both sides of the story, and they need to look at things from our perspective. A lot of time, parents just assume things, and what they think is completely wrong could be right for their kid.*
- *Stop pretending to fit in with the people in your group who are fake, and choose to make a new path.*
- *School assemblies on bullying do not help at all.*
- *I think people need to accept one another for who they are and not for how they look.*
- *I want the world to learn how to feel, listen, and be empathetic. I wish people could understand how important it is to put your eyes on the people who matter most.*
- *Everyone matters.*

The fear of rejection has always been a significant source of stress for adolescents. Not making the team, being left out of a gathering or overlooked for the school play, and feeling alienated or teased by peers are common and often unavoidable exclusions. Many young people today find it more comfortable to interact with peers via text, Snapchat or similar apps, and online gaming rather than face-to-face. The rise in technology usage by those seeking social connection can compound feelings of inadequacy and isolation. Couple this with the unrealistic and superficial standards of beauty and popularity created by and portrayed via social media, and it further magnifies the insecurities of this already awkward phase of life. The unachievable standard can compel young people to hide their true, authentic selves, leading to debilitating consequences for our kids. A study by the Pew Research Center found that only 25 percent of teens spend time with friends in person (outside of school) on a daily basis.[1] While digital communication tools have opened doors to global information sharing and interactions not bound by our physical presence, they come with a downside, especially for teens. Online interaction often heightens FOMO (fear of missing out), creates unrealistic ideals, reduces genuine human interaction, and increases the opportunity for cyberbullying and rumor spreading.

Compounding this crisis is the increased demand on working parents' time outside the office as work expectations via email, messaging, and phone calls intersect with the responsibilities of family life. Parents are combatting many of the same technological distractions faced by their kids, along with the demands and realities of family life. Needless to say, the presence and support the young people in their lives need is often lacking.

The pressure parents feel in their own lives, or the scars they carry from their own childhoods, can lead to distractions that create barriers in the relationships they have with their children. Parents whose fears lead them to define their own success by comparing their children to others or parents who feel compelled to shelter or rescue their children from pain and disappointment send clear messages of "you're not good enough" and "you're not

---

1. Amanda Lenhart, "Teens, Technology and Friendships," Pew Research Center, August 6, 2015, https://www.pewinternet.org/2015/08/06/teens-technology-and-friendships.

capable" to their kids. These messages of rejection are intense and paralyzing to the young people who are on the receiving end.

It's not an easy task for adults to offset the powerful impact of exclusion on the lives of their kids and provide presence and support in the midst of life's demands, but it *is* possible. With awareness of our own struggles and intentional effort, we can equip our kids with the ability to overcome life's rejections, fuel their sense of inner strength, and teach them compassion.

As Truth-tellers, we don't have to hide our insecurities from those who look up to us. Instead, we can choose to model for our young people how to overcome insecurity and grow stronger in spite of rejection. We do this by:

- Reinforcing that they have value—not because of what they do or what they own, but because they are divinely designed to bring unique gifts to the world.
- Encouraging them to see the value in others.
- Teaching them to be an Upstander rather than a bystander by speaking their pain and demonstrating how it can be used to genuinely connect and empathize with others.
- Modeling healthy ways to cope with the uncomfortable feelings that arise from the fear of not being understood or accepted.
- Providing tools that turn pain into purpose after letdown, disappointment, or rejection.

In the pages ahead, we'll explore strategies for nurturing seeds of belonging through three practices: *Pledging, Detecting,* and *Reaching.*

Although I lived most of my adult life feeling rejected due to my own self-judgment, it was not too late to decide I would not pass that pressure on to my children. Perhaps making that shift sounds appealing to you, but you don't know where to start.

I believe it starts when we decide to stop worrying about how our children's appearance, actions, and achievements reflect *on us* and start focusing on how our unconditional love and support reflects *on them*.

> Whether they are
> twirling with joy,
> melting down in frustration,
> or aching with pain,
>> accepting them *as they are* reinforces the inherent belief that
>> they are worthy of belonging, which is stronger than
>> any rejection they will face in the days and years ahead.

BELONGING THROUGH PLEDGING

I can vividly remember times in my life when I have been excluded and rejected. I remember how badly I wanted the rejecters to understand the pain they caused, offer me a genuine apology, and hear them pledge to never do it to anyone else.

That happened only once.

As for the rest of the occurrences, there was either no resolution or no remorse. I walked away feeling hurt, angry, conflicted, and confused.

When my daughters began coming to me with their own hurtful experiences, I felt a familiar wave of unsettledness. In a few cases, there was partial resolution, but most of time, there was no closure at all. The ones who inflicted the pain either lacked remorse or were unaware of the hurt their actions caused, so the effects of their behavior went unacknowledged and unresolved. My daughters were left to process the raw emotions of their experiences with no silver lining of change or reconciliation. While some infractions might seem minor compared to others, repeatedly feeling defeated weighs heavy on the soul.

As a Truth-teller, I vowed not to trivialize my children's feelings, resort to bad-mouthing the rejecter, or shrug off the rejection with tired clichés such as, "It's their loss." I also did not want the rejection to turn into self-blame or inner criticism. I knew what I *didn't* want to do, but having lacked these very skills myself at their age, I had to search for the right perspective to give, which begged the question: What *should* we do when someone rejects us?

Renowned author and speaker for young people, Kari Kampakis, had the answer. In an unforgettable Facebook post, Kari wrote:

> Everyone has something to teach you. And while people who are kind and friendly help teach you who you *do* want to be, those who are not kind and friendly teach you who you *don't* want to be. So when you encounter someone who hurts your feelings, lean into that feeling. Ask yourself what they did to make you feel that way. Was it the words they chose? Their tone? The way they picked favorites and ignored everyone else?
>
> Whatever they did, make a pledge. Promise yourself that you'll never treat anyone the way they treated you. This is how you become a kinder and more compassionate person. This is how you learn from other people's mistakes.
>
> And when you meet someone you really like, lean into that feeling, too. Ask yourself what they did to make you feel so good. Then make a pledge to yourself to be more like them. This is also how you become a kinder and more compassionate person.
>
> Regardless of how anyone treats you, you stand to benefit. While some people teach you who you *do* want to be, others teach you who you *don't* want to be. And it's the people who teach you who you *don't* want to be that provide some of the most lasting and memorable lessons on social graces, human dignity, and the importance of acting with integrity.[2]

---

2. Kari Kampakis, Facebook, July 28, 2017, https://www.facebook.com/kari kampakiswriter/posts/everyone-in-your-life-serves-a-purpose-everyone-has-some thing-to-teach-youand-wh/1274262146033217/, emphases added.

Kari's enlightened perspective was the resolution for which I'd been searching. This perspective—that even hurtful, unresolved experiences can have closure by viewing them as a learning experience and a way to become a better person—was both empowering and liberating.

I knew I'd be using Kari's wisdom in my life, as well as to help guide my daughters in theirs. Little did I know how soon I would need Kari's perspective.

As we were driving home from swim team practice one evening, Avery told me she was troubled by something that had happened at school.

When she informed a close friend that she needed to have surgery, the friend launched into a long list of people who had surgeries that were "worse" than the one Avery was going to have. Avery explained to me that every time she shares either bad news or good news with this particular friend, the friend treats it as a competition and tries to outdo her.

When Avery told her friend about the way her unkind response made her feel, her friend became defensive and angry.

"She walked away mad," Avery said sadly.

I pointed out that a defensive response usually indicates that someone feels insecure, and then I introduced the term "one-uppers" as people who typically have fragile self-esteems and tell others how great they are in an effort to impress.

"But what if you were to see this person who one-ups you as a teacher?" I said. "While she may seem like an unlikely teacher or an unqualified one, see her as someone here to teach you something. What did she teach you today?"

Avery thought for a moment. Then she said, "She taught me to say something comforting when people tell me they are scared or when they share bad news."

"Yes, exactly!" I said. "I'm very sorry you had that experience today. It doesn't sound like your friend is receptive to your feedback, but all hope is not lost—*you* can be the change! Now, when a friend tells you about something bad that's going on in her life, you can respond with the compassion you would have liked to receive today."

Channeling Kari's advice, I told Avery it might be a good idea to make a pledge to herself. When we got home, Avery decided to make an actual pledge book. We both agreed to use it whenever an unlikely teacher taught us something through a hurtful experience.

Some of our pledges include:

I pledge to always ask, "How are you doing?" and to really listen.
I pledge to be honest.
I pledge never to say, "You owe me," after I do something nice
    for someone.
I pledge to support someone's dream, no matter how far-fetched it is.
I pledge to give my full attention when someone is talking to me.
I pledge to consider who I might be excluding.
I pledge to speak up when something is not okay.
I pledge not to dismiss someone's feelings just because I deal with
    things differently or have never personally experienced what she
    is experiencing.
I pledge not to comment on someone's body or weight.
I pledge to say something if I see someone being mistreated.
I pledge not to jump to conclusions.
I pledge to make it easy for people to be themselves around me.

Since starting our pledge book a few years ago, it has grown quite substantial. Taking rejections and turning them into positive intentions is cathartic and empowering. It was helpful for me to revisit some hurtful rejections from my past and transform them into pledges. But I've found that the pledge book has been most relevant during the middle school years. Periods of uncertainty, exclusion, rejection, and insecurity are common during this tumultuous time, especially when our culture is so quick to judge or lambast those with differing opinions. As many kids watch adults reject each other due to differing political and social beliefs, arming them with the truth that they can alter patterns of acceptable social response offers great hope.

I saw it in one of my daughter's pledges. Avery wrote, *I pledge not to call someone a name just because we have a different opinion.*

She had expressed an inclusive opinion and was met with insults and belittling. While the tendency might have been to . . .

lash out
attack
ridicule
argue
unfriend
hold a grudge
gossip
or condemn,

my daughter did something better.
She pledged to stop the hurt rather than perpetuate it.
She pledged to be the change she wanted to see.
She pledged to turn pain into purpose.

And I am seeing it. I am seeing the pledges in her book come to life through her actions and words. And mine, too.

You might even say the pledge book sitting on her dresser is a *Playbook for Bettering Humanity.*

Just imagine for a moment, if we all had one.
When hurtful words are thrown like confetti,
when quick judgments are made in a couple of keystrokes,
when seats are saved and there's no room at the table,

when pain cuts deep and resolution is nowhere near,
we could pause and ask ourselves: *What is this person here to
  teach me?*

And from that unlikely teacher, a painful experience could
become a pledge for more awareness and a ripple of change for all
of humanity.

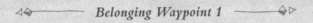

Belonging Waypoint 1

THE TRUTH ABOUT REJECTION

When I receive disapproving messages in my online work, I often
share them with my daughters. Not only is it a good way to avoid
letting the rejection become a source of shame for me, but it
models how I keep showing up to use my gifts, even at the risk
of rejection.

One particular situation I experienced was minor but left a
lasting impression on my daughter, Avery. I'd created a quote meme
for social media, not realizing there was a typo in it. Despite the
misused word, the post resonated with many people and went viral.

I likely would never have known about the typo had it not
been for the person who, later that night, commented, "The
incorrectly used 'the' ruined this."

For a fleeting moment, I felt embarrassed about the mistake.
I was already making my way down the old path of self-judgment
when I reminded myself of this important truth: *Perfection is not
my friend.* From personal experience, I knew that expecting perfection from myself could single-handedly destroy any chance I
had of living out my purpose and experiencing true joy.

I told Avery about the reader's comment. After we had a

good chuckle, I told her I could try to live my life avoiding rejection and disapproval from others, but that would mean playing it safe, allowing my fears to limit my ability to live out my purpose. This notion stuck with her and helped her get through a stressful moment when she was asked to lead the music in children's church the following Sunday.

Right before Avery's debut, she discovered she'd been given the wrong song to practice all week. This meant the room full of young children eager to sing along would not know the words. I saw the fear in Avery's eyes as she looked out into that room, fearing confusion and possibly judgment from the audience. With a deep breath, she began strumming and singing—the wrong song—with her whole heart.

Afterward, Avery described how she felt like crying, but instead told herself, *The message is more important than the mistake.*

Living in fear of rejection and disapproval means cutting ourselves off from connection, growth, healing, and the ability to radiate our divine light. Once kids understand how to break down the fundamental beliefs that fuel feelings of rejection, they are better equipped to see rejection as a part of life that makes us stronger, wiser, and more compassionate.

As the following truths about rejection and belonging present themselves in your own life, take it as an invitation to share them with your kids.

Belonging matters. When kids wonder why feeling rejected hurts so badly and makes them doubt their worth, explain that it is because the deepest desire of the human heart is to belong—to be included and to know you are seen and valued. Everyone has this need; it's what makes us human. That means it's perfectly normal to feel hurt when we are excluded. What is tough to perceive at a young age, though, is that everyone has some form of insecurity about a space they don't fit in, even the most popular, most intelligent, or most athletic people. Some just hide it better than others.

Not everyone will like us. As author Harlan Cohen explains with the "universal rejection truth," not everyone we like will always like us, and that's okay.[3] Not everyone is compatible. Not everyone is looking for the same thing in a friend. Explain how great it feels to "click" with people, when conversation comes easily, and you feel free to be your true self instead of holding back a part of who you are for fear of judgment. We don't always find people with whom we connect right away, but as Truthtellers, we have to assure our kids that it's worth the effort, the patience, and the risk to seek out people like this in our lives.

It's not about you. In a culture that communicates with text messages and Snapchats, feelings of rejection and hopelessness can arise from unresponsiveness. Kids (and adults, too) are often quick to create a false narrative in their heads about why a person is not responding. Share the strategies you use when you extend an invitation or message and it goes unanswered. My kids know that when I don't hear back from a friend, I tell myself, *She must have a lot on her plate.* This perspective stops me from overthinking the lack of response and fills the void with compassion rather than concern.

It's important to be aware that replaying everything you did or said in an attempt to figure out if you did or said something wrong is a waste of precious time and energy. It is not our job to figure out why people do what they do. Our job is to show up as ourselves and put positive energy into the world.

3. Harlan Cohen, "Worried about Rejection," *Harlan Cohen: America's Most Trusted College Life Expert* (blog), February 3, 2009, https://harlancohen.blogspot.com/2009/02/dear-harlan-i-met-this-guy-over.html.

Shift your focus in a new direction. Kids need to know that there may come a point when rejection from a particular person becomes a pattern, making the relationship unhealthy. Give your kids permission to decide they are no longer going to subject themselves to hurtful treatment. Help them navigate how they might create a buffer without making a dramatic exit or involving others. Once they've made the decision to move on from an unhealthy relationship, point out that now they have more time, energy, and love to dedicate to someone or something else. Volunteering at a homeless cat shelter and local nursing home have provided me and my daughters with a place where our love and presence is received without expectation or conditions. Volunteering in any capacity tends to shift our focus away from our current woes and put it instead on our blessings, while bringing purpose to our lives and providing an opportunity for genuine human connection.

BELONGING THROUGH DETECTING

As I was learning to accept all parts of myself, even my insecurities and weaknesses, I made a discovery that allows me to accept my kids in their most vulnerable moments so communication lines stay open and growth can occur in our relationship. The momentous discovery is this: *Fear wears disguises.*

This compassion-igniting gem of truth came to me during a white-water rafting experience in the Blue Ridge Mountains. As my family navigated its first set of raging rapids, I feared Avery was going to fall out. I began calling out orders, sharp and gruff.

"Don't be upset," Scott said.

"I'm not mad; I'm scared!" I declared, holding back tears.

That's when three miraculous words came from my mouth: "That's fear talking."

All at once, I saw the unbecoming behaviors I'd exhibited for decades when I was scared or anxious in a new, forgiving light. I often wondered how I could be so mean to and controlling of people I loved so much. Attributing those unbecoming behaviors to fear of rejection, failure, and loss removed the shame and helped me grow into a more loving, accepting parent who could model healthy emotional regulation.

This enabled me to identify my triggers, which helped me to *catch myself* before I did or said something I would immediately regret. My kids now understood that when I said, "I'm having a hard time right now," I needed them to be quiet and give me space. This verbal cue enabled me to be truthful about painful emotions rather than repress them until I exploded. Not only was I catching myself before hurtful words emerged, but I was figuratively *holding myself* with love and compassion by expressing my uneasiness in a moment of angst.

When I began this truth-telling practice, I hoped it would eventually transfer to my kids. Although they are not yet practicing it consistently, I see signs that they are moving in that direction. Fortunately, the teen years provide plenty of opportunities to practice processing big feelings and unbecoming behaviors through a lens of love.

I recall one morning when Natalie's alarm did not go off, and I could see the stress mounting as she rushed around, trying to get herself together in record time. As every single one of my kind gestures to help her was met with short, cranky responses, I felt my own irritation grow. *Here I am trying to help her, and she is being rude to me!*

In the face of rejection, my brain was flooded with snarky comments. I considered voicing one of them when my heart said, *STOP. Her negative response is not about you—that is fear talking.* Instantly, my heart softened, and I put myself in Natalie's shoes. Walking into class late meant having all eyes on her. Knowing how much my daughter despised being the center of attention, I could feel her fear. As a freshman in high school, I probably would rather have stayed home sick than walk in late to class. But there she was, trying to get ready as fast as she could. If I chose to reject Natalie in that moment by making her response about me, it would only add to her stress. I chose to do what I'd asked my daughters to do when I was feeling vulnerable: I stayed quiet, calm, and steady. *I held myself.*

As we neared the school, I noticed Natalie had clasped her hands together tightly. I wondered if she was using the technique she told me about a few years prior when she signed up for Lunch Bunch, a middle school program where kids could sign up to eat lunch with special education students.

When I'd asked Natalie how lunch went, she'd described how awkward it was at first, but said that eventually she made a connection with one student. When I complimented her on not giving up, she said something I won't soon forget.

"I clasped my hands together so I wouldn't do anything embarrassing. It made me feel calm—like I was holding my own hand. You can hold your own hand and be brave, you know."

I believe that was what she was doing on that hard morning when her alarm did not go off; I was witnessing her personal version of "catching yourself" in a moment of fear and uncertainty.

Then, at last, the vulnerable truth came out. "If I'm late, I'll have to go to the office, and I don't know where it is yet," Natalie said softly.

Before we began talking through a solution, I said a prayer of gratitude. I felt incredibly thankful I'd been able to recognize fear talking earlier that morning, and that doing so had enabled me to step out of the role of judge and into the role of ally. Licensed psychotherapist and author Lisa McCrohan calls this critical skill "decoding," and acknowledges that the messages our young people send us can be difficult to decipher because what they say isn't always what they mean. Through years of work with families in psychotherapy and coaching, Lisa concludes that what young people are most often asking for in their difficult moments is acceptance. "Our kids may not have the words to say exactly what they need; they may not even know exactly what they are feeling or thinking; they just want to know they are loved and that you will stand by them."[4]

As our teens exhibit unbecoming behaviors and attitudes, it would serve us well to remember that fear and anxiety often present themselves as defensiveness, sarcasm, control, and unkindness. When these characteristics are present, it is not a call for us to expose fault, lash back, ignore, or lecture, but rather a call to love.

Choosing a steady response to our child's deepest fears opens the door to connection. This allows us to respond to their pain in ways we couldn't before. From there, anything is possible.

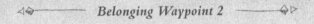

Belonging Waypoint 2

THE REASONABILITY TEST

Inevitably, life gets unstable at times. We can be going along just fine, and then out of the blue, we're thrown off kilter. Suddenly, everything we thought we knew feels shaky and uncertain. In my family's life, instability was the theme of spring 2017. The unexpected loss of a parent and grandfather, teenage hormonal changes, friendship turmoil, and academic adjustments contributed to an unstable environment and emotional challenges that

4. Lisa McCrohan, "Decoding Your Teen: Understanding Your Teen's Subtle Bid for Connection," *Lisa McCrohan* (blog), November 7, 2019, https://www.lisamccrohan .com/2019/11/decoding-your-teen-understanding-your-teens-subtle-bid-for-connection -and-how-to-respond-with-presence-and-compassion/.

threatened to put my reactive mode into overdrive. But during that time, I decided to observe my feelings without reacting and to practice being aware and honest with myself. I made another incredible breakthrough. I realized:

> Anxiety in the people I love makes me want to control.
> Sassiness in the people I love makes me want to get defensive.
> Pain in the people I love makes me want to rescue.
> Silence in the people I love makes me want to shut down.

But those responses from me are not helpful or healing; in fact, they only add to the chaos and make the situation worse. What *is* helpful and healing is to provide what is lacking in the situation: *stability*.

When a loved one is in distress, I am called to be steady—to respond consistently and calmly with love, understanding, and compassion, regardless of what is coming at me. This is not easy, but it is possible. What keeps me in check is something I call The Reasonability Test. I use this test to help me be a calming presence in an emotionally tense moment or period. The Reasonability Test is most helpful when I'm met with pushback and conflict is quickly escalating. That's when I check in with myself using the following three questions:

> *Is what I am asking or saying reasonable?*
> *Do I sound like a voice of reason?*
> *Does my body language match my calm voice and words?*

If the answer to any of these questions is *no*, there's a good chance I'm contributing to the instability and conflict. I make adjustments to my words, tone, body language, and/or expectations so I can better understand and be better understood.

If the answer to any of the three questions is *yes*, and the other person is not responding reasonably, it most likely means there is a deeper issue at hand.

That's when I offer one of three reasonable solutions—help, validation, or space—to get to the root of the issue.

> **Help:** "I know you are under a lot of stress right now, how can I help?"
>
> **Validation:** "You really wanted it to work out differently. I am so sorry it didn't work out that way."
>
> **Space:** "I'm going to give you some time to yourself. I'll be right out here if you need me. Perhaps in a bit we can talk about why you're so upset."

To a scared soul, these options feel like comfort.

To a drowning mind, these options feel like oxygen.

To a rejected heart, these options feel like acceptance.

We may not have the ability to improve our loved ones' situation or remedy the problem, but we can hold their moving world steady long enough for them to get their footing. With our loving support, we provide balance to stay on track, no matter what tries to derail us.

BELONGING THROUGH REACHING

When we moved to a new state five years ago, my prayer was for one friend for each of my kids—one good, solid, loyal, and loving friend. Natalie found that friend quite quickly. Avery's path to friendship was, and still is, a bit more complex. Being a Noticer, she has a keen awareness of other people's struggles and fears. She feels pain deeply and expresses it honestly. She is a master at making others feel seen, heard, and known—which is most likely why it is so painful when she feels invisible and disregarded. Moving to a new area and leaving all that is familiar proved especially traumatic, and for many months, Avery's school days ended in tears.

I can't remember exactly when Avery stopped saying, "I want to go back home." Did it take twelve months? Fifteen? Twenty-one? I don't know. For a while, Avery's heart teetered back and forth between the place she came from and the place she was trying to embrace. Although I can't pinpoint the moment she stopped longing for "home," I am certain of three things: we anticipated it, we talked about it, and we looked forward to it with expectancy. The hope I offered was always rooted in truth—that it was possible to find that *one* true friend, and that it would not necessarily happen as a result of luck or chance, but because of effort and awareness, and by taking risks.

"Tell me the 'look for her' story again," Avery often said during these months when our conversations centered on the topic of friendship.

Avery was referring to the friendship that was born out of my worst-ever birthday—one of the loneliest, most desolate times of my life. Scott and I had just moved to a small town on the eastern shore of Mobile, Alabama, with our two young daughters. I'd left behind a loving support system in Florida, which included my parents. As a result, I was depressed, anxious, sleep-deprived, and lonely.

On my birthday, I had to go to the grocery store for milk and bread. As the girls and I embarked on our errand, I remember looking in every car as we traveled, down every grocery store aisle as we shopped, and in every house as we pulled into our neighborhood. Not one familiar face. Not one person in this city to smile at me and say, "Happy birthday," because we knew no one. On that birthday, I realized I needed something far more than milk and bread.

In my desperation, I searched online for local moms' groups. Much to my relief, there was a meeting coming up. Again, I strapped my daughters in their car seats and scanned faces as we traveled. But this time I didn't look for *familiar*—instead, I looked for *friendly*. I found it in the face of a woman named Courtney, when she held the door for me and my girls to enter the building.

I'll never forget the first invitation I received from her after the meeting. She called and said, "A group of us are meeting at the park with our kids. Why don't you join us?" I cried with relief. And for the remainder of the year that we lived in that city, Courtney made sure I did not walk alone.

Two moves later, my daughters had grown too old for me to drop in on moms' groups or strike up impromptu swing set conversations with would-be friends. Yet the memory of my worst birthday and wandering the grocery aisles looking for something familiar to latch onto motivated me to stretch beyond my comfort zone to make my birthday special this time. I noticed that one of my favorite authors, Glennon Doyle, was coming to speak in a nearby city the day before my birthday. I bought a ticket and garnered the courage to take my directionally-challenged self on an hour-long drive during rush hour to attend the event by myself.

I remember experiencing the most incredible phenomenon while listening to Glennon speak in a packed church sanctuary that night. I did not know a soul, but through Glennon's honest words and the energy of the sisterhood around me, I didn't feel alone; I felt connected.

As I was leaving to go home, a woman called out, "Hands-Free Mama!" When I turned, I saw two women, one with tears running down her cheeks. The woman who approached me introduced her friend, Megan, who wanted to thank me for writing messages that had helped her family. When she found it difficult to speak, I wrapped my arms around her and just held on. This beautiful woman went on to become one of my dearest friends in the city where I now live.

Although Megan was unusually unresponsive to my invitations for a six-month spell during our friendship, I continued to support her through messages and calls. I did not take her lack of response as rejection; I took it as a sign that she might be dealing with something I knew nothing about. One day, after months of silence, Megan and I met at a park. After sharing the details of an ongoing struggle I could never have imagined, Megan said something I will never forget: *Thank you for not giving up on me.*

Avery's response to my worst-birthday-ever story has always reflected the same enduring persistence I had to employ in order to find a real friend: "I won't stop looking for her."

But as young people often do, Avery took the seed of hope I'd given her and sprinkled it with a fresh dose of optimism, courage, and resourcefulness, which eventually blossomed into her finding the *one* friend for whom she hoped and prayed.

It was their matching smiles that initially drew them to each other, but they soon found they shared a love of singing. In time, a beautiful friend-duo emerged. I loved watching how they honored their differences and made a point to see situations from one another's perspectives. Whether it was Laila being unable to eat gluten or Avery having to wear glasses or either girl having to navigate cliques in school, they each made sure the other never felt less-than or left out. Avery and Laila's friendship knew no judgment, only whole-hearted attempts to understand—through sharing experiences—what they could not possibly know without the beautiful perspective their friendship provided.

I'll never forget the day Avery came home after school unusually upset. I suspected she was going to say she was homesick, as she had done for so many months. But as soon as she spoke, I actually wished homesickness was the reason for her distress.

Avery reported that a boy on the bus had made a racist comment to Laila.

I began to shake with anger. "What did you do?" I asked as calmly as I could.

"I asked Laila if she was okay. She didn't say anything, so I just scooted closer." Wiping tears from her eyes, Avery admitted, "I didn't know what to do, so I just hurt with her."

I hurt with her.

It took me a moment to recover from that.

"Thank you for standing with your friend," I said. I then told her I must also do something. I immediately notified the school principal. Expressing deep concern, the principal assured both my daughter and me that swift action would be taken.

The next day, Avery reported that her teacher had unexpectedly walked the girls onto the bus. With her arms protectively around my child and her friend, the long-time educator announced to the boy and those seated around him, "You mess with my girls, you mess with me."

"My friend felt stronger and less worried after that," Avery said. "My teacher had our back."

I noticed Avery had said, "our" back, not "her" back.

This notion of standing with and walking beside one another reinforced to me the importance of embracing my role as Truthteller for my twenty-first-century kid. It's not enough to tell our kids to be kind, inclusive, and to *look for* potential friends; Avery's honest recounting of her willingness to see her friend's pain, and to be there with her in it, solidified my belief that we must *show* our kids how to truly *see* everyone we encounter. This means having honest conversations about what to do if they see someone being bullied, alienated, or mistreated. This means having open dialogue about topics that run the gamut from harassment in the school hallways to systems of oppression in the wider world. This means modeling through our words and actions what it looks like to be respectful of races, cultures, and religions different from our own. This means *being* the friend, ally, and confidant we want to have. This means encouraging our kids to be helpers, but perhaps even more importantly, to also be listeners.

Some of the deepest forms of rejection involve the dismissal of someone's pain because we ourselves have never experienced it. If we choose to not "get involved" because the situation makes us uncomfortable, we will not experience the compassion that comes from understanding who someone truly is, what matters most to them, and what mountain they are trying to climb.

Krystle Cobran, story weaver, teacher, and author of *The Brave Educator: Honest Conversations About Navigating Race in the Classroom*, started a business to help people talk about race in a way that builds connection and belonging instead of division and exclusion. Krystle believes the heart of this peaceable connection is listening. She writes:

> I've been thinking about a myth that goes something like this: *I can know who you are by standing on the outside and judging you by what I think I know.* I let this myth control my life, my conversations, for longer than I want to admit to you. It took a long time, but eventually, I decided the cost was too high. The cost was losing sight of your humanity. And my own.
>
> The truth is that I need to listen to you in order to see you. I need to crave an understanding of who you are, be willing to remember that you have tender places so that we can really connect.
>
> Standing on the outside and passing judgment was convenient, but it was entirely too painful to bear. Too many people forgotten, too many stories unheard. Too many human beings reduced to boxes.

It's challenging to choose connection and listening over judgment, but the beauty of seeing another human being for who they are, even just for a moment, is worth it.[5]

Krystle's world-changing approach can start at home when we choose to see our kids for who they are—not for who we *want* them to be. When we acknowledge that our kids' thoughts, feelings, voices, and experiences hold value, they are better equipped to extend that same understanding to the people they encounter, despite their differences and no matter what those differences are.

I believe these four questions, inspired by Krystle, Laila, and Avery, have the potential to help us build an inclusive mind-set that leads to greater acceptance and belonging:

- What if we responded to the injustices inflicted on human lives with empathy, rather than defensiveness, apathy, or indifference?
- What if we embraced the notion that the freedom, opportunities, and resources held by some would be far greater if shared by all?
- What if we practiced "hurting with" as a starting point when we don't know what to do for someone in pain?
- What if we lived as if we truly believed it's not "your back" or "my back," but "our back"?

If we are to create a more just and peaceful world for future generations, let us keep looking around with open eyes, ears, and hearts so we can begin to truly *see* the potential of *us*.

---

5. Krystle Cobran, "How to Help People Feel Seen and Heard When the Whole World Feels Tired, Exhausting, and Filled with Fear," *Krystle Cobran Story Weaver* (blog), https://krystlecobran.com/new-blog/2020/1/how-to-help-people-feel-seen-and-heard-when-the-whole-world-feels-tired-exhausting-and-filled-with-fear.

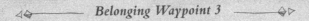

Belonging Waypoint 3

BE AN UPSTANDER

An online reader of my blog wrote to tell me that her daughter, a high school student, noticed the damaging impact of the way teams were chosen in P.E. class. Each day, the teacher selected two of the most popular girls as captains and let them choose their teammates one by one. Having seen the pain, rejection, and stress this caused her classmates, and having felt it herself, this young woman decided to do something about it.

With her permission to share, this is what the young lady wrote to her teacher:

> I have noticed that when the two captains pick teams, it always leaves people feeling bad because they are picked last, including myself sometimes. I ask you to change the method of picking teams, so no one has to feel bad in a mandatory gym class some may not already like. I hope you understand.

The teacher's response was encouraging. After thanking the young woman for advocating for herself and others, she outlined several fair, equitable, and dignified ways they would identify teams from that day forward.

If this seems like a small thing, consider the impact. From now on, when it is time to pick teams, no one will stand there waiting in pain. No one will hold their breath, hoping this time might be different. No one will wish they were so small that the floor could swallow them up. For the first time in many agonizing months—perhaps years—the activity of picking teams will no longer result in the pain caused by rejection. These are no small things. Just imagine the impact on our world if our kids learned to advocate for each other the way this brave high school sophomore did for her peers!

In our roles as Truth-tellers, we can instill an empowering hope in our kids: *You are not helpless against suffering, cruelty, and hopelessness; you simply need to open your eyes and use whatever means you have to bring awareness to someone's situation.*

We can start by telling our kids there is a word for people who do this: *Upstander.*

Believing that words have the power to influence the choices people make, two New Jersey high school students, Monica Mahal and Sarah Decker, began a campaign to get the word *upstander* (as opposed to bystander) added to the dictionary. They wanted to give a name to behavior that is crucial for building stronger communities and a more humane world. As a result of this campaign, *upstander* was added to the *Oxford English Dictionary* in 2016.

The following characteristics of an Upstander from an organization called Generations Against Bullying (GAB) can help kids identify how to assume this world-changing role. Upstanders are those who:

- ask the outliers on the sidelines to join in the game
- make space at the lunch table for someone sitting alone
- make sure everyone is included in the group
- smile at others in the hallways and say hello to the people who need it the most
- ask questions when they seek to understand the world around them
- yearn to know the "why" and the "how come"
- choose to act, even when it is not convenient, easy, or safe

Generations Against Bullying believes that today's parents have the opportunity to raise an entire generation of Upstanders by pointing out real-life examples, letting kids ask hard questions, and honoring historic figures such as Martin Luther King Jr., Nelson Mandela, Dietrich Bonhoeffer, and Mahatma Gandhi, all of whom made their mark on history as Upstanders.[6]

I believe it, too.

One day, our kids will cross paths with someone who can't bear one more rejection, one more heartbreak, one more day alone. How beautiful that our kids can ease the pain by saying, "I see you. Come be on my team. Together is better."

One person can do that.

LIVE LOVE NOW REFLECTION: WE ALL HOLD KEYS

The black shoes were what I saw first.

I was on the floor of the cat shelter room taking photos of Hickory, a big orange cat who loves his freedom from the cage, when a teenager walked up to the floor-to-ceiling window.

He was dressed in black from head to toe and wore a solemn expression. I watched as his eyes went from one cage to the other, as if inspecting each animal.

Skeptical thoughts entered my mind.

Wait, my heart said. *Don't assume the worst. Maybe the young man is looking for a specific kind of cat to adopt, or perhaps he's lost one.*

I quickly reminded myself that when onlookers come to the cat shelter window while my daughters and I are cleaning, we always peek out the door and ask if there's a particular cat they are interested in seeing.

Why would you not do it now? my heart questioned.

---

6. For more information about Generations Against Bullying, visit gabnow.org.

I got up from the floor and peered out. "Is there a particular cat you are interested in seeing?"

"No. I just love cats," the young man said, robotically and unsmiling.

Instantly, I was transported back in time. I was with one of my special education students. He had loved cats, too, yet he'd harmed his own in an emotional episode.

When his mom told me what he'd done, I was shocked, saddened, angered, heartbroken. I didn't know how I would ever be able to work with him again.

The day after the incident, my student asked to see me. He asked if I knew what he'd done, my cat calendar hanging on the wall just behind his head. It was undoubtedly one of the hardest conversations of my life.

A cat's meow stirred me from my reverie, and I returned to the present moment. Standing outside the shelter door was a young man who loved cats, and I had the keys.

I opened the door again.

"Would you like to play with the cats? They love when someone runs the stick with the mouse along the cages," I said.

"Yes," the teenager said without making eye contact. With large steps, he quickly closed the distance between us.

For ten minutes, the visitor flicked the toy stick back and forth across the cages. When the kitten pair, Elvis and Presley, scaled their cages to get their little claws and mouths on the toy, the boy's face broke into a wide smile. My daughters and I smiled, too.

When I asked the young man if he had cats at home, he told us about his two rescue cats, including their names, colorings, and breeds. Never once did he make eye contact.

Eventually, a woman came up to the window. I can't be sure it was his mother, but the gratitude in her eyes was unmistakable.

"I have to go," said the teen, gently replacing the toy back on the shelf.

He did not say thank you, but for the first time, he looked into my eyes. And when he did, I felt a connection that brought peace to my soul.

After he left, I felt so grateful for his presence, so grateful I hadn't assumed the worst. The encounter served as a powerful reminder that . . .

We all hold keys.
We all can give opportunities.
We all can provide shelter.
Why we don't—well, there are many reasons:
fear
ego
greed
distractedness
prejudice
past experience
to name just a few.
I am guilty of withholding keys.

But that young man reminded me, just as my former student had, that our job is not to be anyone's judge and jury; our job is to love, to invite, to connect—especially and most importantly when the person standing in front of us is shut out and we hold keys.

Several years after I stopped teaching, I heard from my former student. "You were the only one," he said, "the only one who didn't write me off that day."

In my mind, I returned to that moment, when he'd sat in my office with pleading eyes. I'd had no idea what to say to him. And then, five unexpected words came out of my dry mouth: "I still believe in you."

Why did I say those words? Not because I am a noble person. In truth, I only said what I would have wanted someone to say to me in my moment of complete shame and isolation. I would have wanted someone to look at me without judgment. I would have wanted someone to look at me and not see the worst in me—to see the *hope* in me.

Little did I know that my words of belief in this young man would become a key he used to make better choices, and eventually, a better life for himself.

It only takes a little bit of noticing to see that many kids are hurting these days—and adults, too. I believe that noticing each other's pain and assuming the best, rather than the worst, might be a good place to begin healing.

With just a small shift in perspective, monumental things happen:

We open doors.

We look into each other's eyes.

We connect as human beings.

We shelter one another.

We include and we accept, just as we would want someone to do for us.

REFLECTION QUESTIONS

1. What are some ideals you have for yourself and/or your kids that make life harder?
2. If you were to release yourself from the role of evaluator, what do you fear might result? What might you gain?
3. How might you reinforce the value and worth of the young people in your life without using external measures or societal definitions of success?
4. What would it look like if you loved yourself or the kids in your life unconditionally? How might you make one of those ideas a reality today?
5. Name one "key" you hold and describe how you might use it to open a door for someone you love.

PART 2

BE AN ENCOURAGER, NOT AN ENFORCER

Encouragers...

- Recognize the effort, growth, character, and/or feelings of others, as opposed to their achievements or their performance.
- Allow others to explore and articulate their feelings and thoughts freely and completely.
- Resist the urge to protect or rescue others from failure, defeat, pain, and letdowns, and instead point out strengths, progress, and inherent value when loved ones encounter trying times.
- Don't just look at results; acknowledge people's intentions as an authentic representation of who they really are, even if their actions didn't result in a positive outcome.
- Accept that human beings are not designed to navigate life alone, and lead by example in asking for support and bravely admitting when you are struggling.
- Consistently offer words of assurance, taking note of the specific kind of affirmations that best fuel the souls of their loved ones. They know that kids especially feed on encouragement and help them through troubling times with reassuring phrases:

> *You are loved.*
> *You are worthy.*
> *You are enough.*
> *You are doing the best you can.*
> *You are capable.*
> *I believe in you.*

CHAPTER 3

ADRIFT

Perhaps the most important thing we ever give each other is our attention.

—Rachel Naomi Remen, *Kitchen Table Wisdom*

On many afternoons, a fourth grader in our neighborhood greets Avery on her way home from the bus stop.

"Hello, Avery," the boy says, stopping in the middle of his kickball game with friends. "How was your day at middle school?" he asks, patiently waiting to hear her reply.

The reason I know this is not because I see it; I know this only because my daughter told me. My perceptive girl knows this is a rare and noteworthy gesture in our fast-paced, head-down, inwardly focused culture.

But it's what Avery said next that stuck with me. She said, "He's one of those people who won't change when he gets a phone."

This insightful observation comes from a young person who has witnessed several before-and-after scenarios related to phone acquisition among her peers. Here are some of the changes she's noticed:

Decreased conversation
Diminished focus
Shortened attention
Missed cues
Reduced empathy
In some instances, personality changes

Avery's observations align with current research on the negative impact smartphones have on emotional well-being and relationships. Although I've read every study on "technoference" I can get my hands on, I have yet to discover anything I haven't already observed firsthand. Once you've lived life tethered to your phone, you are painfully familiar with the symptoms, the damage, and the cost.

Perhaps that's why what I call "the phone effect" is so noticeable to my daughter. For two solid years of her young life, Avery experienced the painful phenomenon of living right next to someone yet feeling invisible.

It all started out so innocently. Technology was my go-to as I completed teaching re-certification coursework online, managed excessive commitments in a new community, and numbed the pain of homesickness. But what began as a way to remain on top of things and escape reality from time to time became habitual behavior.

Before I knew what hit me, I was a moody, distracted, stressed out, critical observer of life, missing all the moments that truly mattered.

It took several years of misery, one painful truth from Scott, a look of fear in Natalie's eyes, and an emotional breakdown to acknowledge the true cost of my highly distracted life. With certainty, I knew that if I continued on this course, my relationships, my health, and my life's ambitions would be damaged beyond repair.

I'll never forget the first step I took to take my life back from technology's addictive grip.

I was in the middle of making lunch when I noticed then-four-year-old Avery sitting on the couch. For the first time in a long time, I noticed her—really noticed her.

Despite the dinging notifications on my phone, the open browsers on my laptop, and the mile-long to-do list staring me down, I knew I had to go and hold my child. Spurring me on was a profound sense of urgency—like time was running out—and there was nothing more important than being with her right then.

After holding her close for several minutes, Avery did something completely unexpected. She picked up my hand and kissed my palm.

It was a moment that changed me forever. It brought my well-intended tirades, over-scheduled life, and the constantly regenerating expectations I had for myself and others into focus with new perspective. I knew I had to take action.

How can I correct the damaging course I am on and start grasping the moments that matter?

With a little divine intervention, the answer soon became clear: *Let go of what* doesn't *matter, so you can grasp what* does.

The solution seemed pretty simple to identify, but it was fundamentally more challenging to implement. I had to let go of the imaginary measuring stick I had created, outlining which actions, achievements, and material possessions added up to success. I had to relieve myself of the stress of over-commitment, the fear of judgment, and the need for approval based on productivity. More important, I had to retrain my mind and body to perceive the actions of those around me as representations of their true selves, not of me. They were each walking to the beat of their own special tune, so who was I to dictate the speed, style, or cadence of the music? These were their gifts, not problems that needed to be fixed, and I needed to remember that and respond accordingly when we encountered future obstacles. I needed space and time to breathe, and I was fairly certain my loved ones did, too.

I immediately designated several "hands-free" time periods

throughout the day—times when I put away the phone, the computer, and the need to be connected to the outside world so I could be fully present with someone I loved.

I didn't realize it then, but I was creating boundaries. *I was teaching myself how to limit my availability to the world so I could be available to those who are my world.*

Almost immediately, I noticed a positive impact on my relationships, as well as on my mental and emotional well-being. By establishing distraction-free periods in the morning, during greetings and departures, at mealtimes and bedtime, I was able to see, hear, and respond more lovingly to my family and to myself. No longer dictated by the dinging demands of devices, my thoughts and actions were my own. I felt less divided and more whole, able to focus on what mattered most to me. I felt anchored.

It seemed only natural to voice these important discoveries to the people I loved, but I didn't want to demand participation. Instead, I wanted to share in a way that empowered and encouraged them to come along on this journey with me.

Instead of saying, "We don't bring electronic devices to the dinner table," I tried saying, "We'll miss out on really tasting our food and enjoying each other's company if we're staring at our screens."

Instead of, "Put away your iPad while we wait for the doctor," I said, "Waiting time is an opportunity to catch up with each other; tell me the best part of your day."

Rather than demanding that all devices be kept in a public area of our house with no explanation, I talked about internet safety and why it was important to keep each other accountable and not hide scary, hurtful, or confusing online situations from each other.

Rather than letting the smile on the cashier's face go unnoticed, I said to my daughters, "Did you see how happy it made the cashier when we acknowledged her instead of looking at a phone while she rang up our items?"

Talking to my daughters regularly and conversationally about the importance of having a time and place for technology became a way of life—just like talking about drugs and alcohol, puberty, body safety and consent, bullying, and other critical topics. This meant I didn't wait until there was a problem with my kids' technology usage to talk about it. Thus, when we did encounter a problem, we already had an established line of communication, and we could work through it together. This proactive and positive approach put me in the role of Encourager, not enforcer. I wanted my kids to see me as someone who was helping them locate their anchor, someone they could count on to walk *beside* them as we navigated this tricky territory *together*.

Finding our way through this ever-changing terrain has not happened without missteps or difficulties, but we've managed to keep our intentions aligned, even when the path is unclear. I want my kids to remain anchored in the understanding that technology is a useful tool, but to be aware that it can also cast a foggy shadow over the real world, that it is a virtual environment loaded with temptations that can cause us to waste time and drift into damaging and potentially addictive behaviors. Young people today are consuming technology at an alarming rate, seemingly to escape reality, and I believe they do so because they lack an anchor, which leads to undue stress and feeling untethered and out of control.

My concerns are confirmed when I speak to young people during my classroom author talks. When I speak candidly about my phone addiction and how it negatively impacted my well-being and my relationships, I can practically hear a pin drop. But when I engage kids in the Index Card Exercise, the evidence is unequivocal—the pervasiveness of technology is creating extreme stress, anxiety, and disconnection in the lives of our kids.

- *One thing my family is missing is time. Time is the only thing we're running out of and can never get back. We need more time so our family can get to know us more and we can make more memories.*

- *I wish parents and adults would listen to what kids have to say. They seem too busy and distracted to talk to us.*
- *The most hurtful thing about technology is seeing all the things I wasn't invited to after I asked people to do something with me and they said they were busy. They weren't that busy, I guess.*
- *Teenagers want to be able to talk to their parents, but parents have to show their kids that they can trust them first.*
- *Parents, go outside with your teens. Take them somewhere peaceful, like a waterfall, or just sit out in the woods and listen to the quiet together.*
- *I deleted Instagram because all it ever showed was how much more fun, cool, and popular everyone was than me. I got rid of it and felt better. I haven't been on it for five months, and I don't even care what goes on there anymore.*
- *I have several secret accounts that my parents don't know about. I wish I didn't have to hide so much of my life, but my parents don't understand, and I don't think they really want to.*
- *I stay up until 3 a.m. most nights, checking my phone to make sure no one is talking bad about me.*
- *Attention. That's what I want most from my parents.*
- *Technology is nothing compared to how powerful caring for each other can be. I wish we could get social media out of our lives so we could focus on the people around us.*
- *Most adults don't understand why a lot of kids get caught up in video games. It's because they want to escape the reality of their lives.*
- *People really need to take time to do things as a family.*

I think we can all agree that today's young people are facing issues no previous generation has ever faced. The tech revolution has changed the way young people socialize, learn, sleep, and perceive the world. With smartphones, instant messaging, and social networking, teens feel they are always "on," and that there is always something they should be doing to become more attractive and likable. Due to the reach and shareability of the online world, normal adolescent stumbles are magnified, publicized, and nearly impossible to escape. Trying to meet school, work, sports, and family expectations while also filtering constant interruptions, managing online identities, and keeping up with streaming communication is causing many young people to feel vulnerable, insecure, ill-equipped, and adrift. They have no anchor.

Even with some level of awareness about the challenges of the digital world, most young people still see their phones as essential, an extension of their existence that must be monitored in real-time. And whether we like it or not, technology is and will be a part of our kids' lives. Yes, we can delay the acquisition of the phone; and yes, we can confiscate their devices and put limits, restrictions, and safeguards on them, but the reality is that kids will find a way to access technology with or without us. By choosing to navigate this uncharted territory with our kids, we place ourselves in a vital position—we become a respected ally who can offer awareness and healthy boundaries for technology. From this position as a model of self-regulation, we can help our kids learn skills that will anchor and ground them—potentially for the rest of their lives—to what really matters and help them let go of what doesn't.

In this fast-paced, head-down, inwardly-focused culture, anchoring our kids by helping them establish healthy tech/life boundaries is undoubtedly one of the most valuable tools we can provide. In our role as Encourager, we can make this happen in several ways:

- By being truthful and sharing our own struggles and triumphs with technology while also acknowledging theirs
- By educating ourselves on the latest research regarding digital wellness and sharing these important findings with our kids without shame, judgment, or hypocrisy

- By teaching our kids mindful tech usage habits so they can learn to hold themselves accountable
- By regularly inviting our kids to join us in real-life activities that fuel our souls, our relationships, and our passions in ways online interactions cannot

In the pages ahead, we'll consider how we might support our kids through these three strategies: *Empowerment*, *Invitation*, and *Protection*.

Although I began my Hands-Free journey eight years ago because I didn't want to miss my life, I also encouraged my children to not miss theirs. Only time will tell if my kids will use the healthy boundaries our family established as they continue to grow, but one thing is certain: the awareness my kids have been given will never leave them.

Although we, as adults, have not experienced a digital childhood, we can be the first generation of parents and educators who show our kids what it looks like to be present participants in a distracted world. We can show our kids that by anchoring ourselves to what lives, breathes, and grows, we can actually experience life while we are living it.

I've learned that it's not as simple as enforcing the powering down of their devices; we must do the hard work of empowering them to choose what really matters. And sometimes that requires the even harder work of being the person who makes those choices first.

By being Encouragers, not enforcers, we offer our kids an antidote to drifting. By encouraging and modeling for our kids how to protect themselves, find their tethers, and accept invitations to choose real life experiences over screens, we equip them with anchors they can cling to when feelings of emptiness and despair creep in, when they are overcome by the fear of missing out, or when they don't know what else to do with their time.

ANCHORING THROUGH EMPOWERMENT

Scott and I purchased a smartphone for Natalie when she began participating in a massive year-round swimming program in a city where we knew no one. Although I felt relieved that she could contact us if practice released early or in case of an emergency, I felt unsettled by the capabilities and risks the device opened up for her. We immediately implemented the recommended online safety guidelines, installed content filtering software, and discussed cyber dangers such as online bullying, predators, pornography, sexting, and what to do in each situation. Still, my uneasiness persisted. I continued to read extensively on the subject and was, for some reason, particularly drawn to articles about teen suicide as they related to social media use.

One night, the uneasiness I'd been feeling reached an all-time high and spurred me to action—preventative action I'd not taken before.

I'd been contacted by two friends from places our family had previously lived whose daughters were in the same grade as Natalie. These vibrant young women with whom she had once played LEGOs and shared towels during swim meets were now harming themselves, hating themselves; the light was dimming from their spirits right in front of their parents' eyes.

After learning about their struggles, I read a sobering article in *Time* magazine about an outgoing young woman named Nina Langton, who shocked everyone with an attempted suicide. The particular details of her story gave me great pause:

> After her attempted suicide and during her stay at a rehabil-
> itation facility, Nina and her therapist identified body image
> insecurity as the foundation of her woe. "I was spending a
> lot of time stalking models on Instagram, and I worried a
> lot about how I looked," says Nina, who is now 17. She'd
> stay up late in her bedroom, looking at social media on her

phone, and poor sleep—coupled with an eating disorder—gradually snowballed until suicide felt like her only option. "I didn't totally want to be gone," she says. "I just wanted help and didn't know how else to get it."[1]

Despite her professional background in public health, Nina's mom, Christine Langton, was caught off-guard by her daughter's suicide attempt. "Nina was funny, athletic, smart, personable," she said. "Depression was just not on my radar."

In hindsight, Langton says she wishes she had done more to moderate her daughter's smartphone use. "It didn't occur to me not to let her have the phone in her room at night," she said. "I just wasn't thinking about the impact of the phone on her self-esteem or self-image until after everything happened."

Nina sounded a lot like my highly driven, very lovable, athletically gifted brown-eyed girl. With that recognition, I knew exactly what I needed to do about the uneasiness I'd been feeling since we gave Natalie a smartphone.

I went to my daughter's room and asked her if we could talk. I felt my heart racing at the importance of the conversation we were about to have. Natalie was stretched out on her bed, surrounded by homework and scrolling Instagram.

I sat down and told Natalie about the two mothers who'd reached out to me for help. My daughter's face fell as I told her about her former teammate, who discovered her looks had been rated on Instagram. I relayed some of the painful comments this young woman had read that had caused her to harm herself. I explained that she'd expressed hating herself so much that she no longer wanted to live.

I then read aloud the eye-opening statistics from a study by

---

1. Markham Heid, "We Need to Talk about Kids and Smartphones," *Time*, October 10, 2017, https://time.com/4974863/kids-smartphones-depression/.

Dr. Jean Twenge, author of *iGen*, that were included in the *Time* magazine article:

> Using data collected between 2010 and 2015 from more than 500,000 adolescents nationwide, Twenge's study found kids who spent three hours or more a day on smartphones or other electronic devices were 34 percent more likely to suffer at least one suicide-related outcome—including feeling hopeless or seriously considering suicide—than kids who used devices two hours a day or less. Among kids who used electronic devices five or more hours a day, 48 percent had at least one suicide-related outcome.

"I'm worried," I told Natalie truthfully. "And it's my job to protect you," I added.

Natalie assured me she had good friends, a sensible head on her shoulders, and would come to me if anything was wrong.

At that point, it would have been easy to end the conversation, have faith everything would be okay, and walk out of the room. It would have been convenient to reduce the screen limit setting on her phone or to just confiscate it all together. Instead, I chose to do the hard thing: I chose to be the Encourager she needed me to be, the person who empowers her with the vital information she needs to navigate this media-saturated world.

The anchor was there; I just had to help her lower it safely into the water, so I offered the following:

I know you are a smart, capable, and resourceful young woman, and those are innate qualities you will call upon time and time again in your life. Those instincts will serve as a compass when the wind is behind you, and they will guide you to safety in rough waters. Unfortunately, the part I can't teach you is how to trust them.

I want you to know it's natural to go through difficult periods when you don't feel like yourself, when you question your worth, when your purpose is not clear. During those times of uncertainty and self-doubt, I want you to use your instincts to reset your perspective and reaffirm your beautiful worth and extraordinary potential.

It's important to understand how others manipulate us when we are online. Social media developers know how to create algorithms to capture and influence our consumption, tap into our insecurities, and ultimately engage further action, such as making a purchase. The goal is to achieve the highest possible amount of engagement in the form of Likes, shares, and follows. There is even a term for this in Silicon Valley: brain hacking. Sadly, these tactics have a negative impact on our mental health—and teenagers are especially susceptible. Here's why.

The teen brain isn't done forming, and the part of the brain that manages impulse control, empathy, judgment, and the ability to plan ahead are not fully developed. This means you're more likely to stumble upon disturbing online content or find yourself in troubling situations; it means you're more likely to become distracted from the important tasks at hand; it means you're more likely to become addicted to your device.

So let's think about this in terms of your life.

Each time the phone alerts you to something, you stop what you are doing, whether it's homework or a job you have to do. What used to take you one hour to do might now take you several hours, and it's safe to assume the work won't be completed as well, thanks to the distraction. Constant distraction will lead to an inability to focus, which will reflect in your grades and impact the job opportunities you have as you grow. Spending quality time with friends and family will be impacted by the need to check for updates, making you believe your phone is most important, instead of the people right in front of you.

Every time you aimlessly scroll, you are being influenced by what you see on the screen. Your thoughts and beliefs about what your body or your life should look like are being shaped. The hidden influence of this exposure can create a poor self-image, unrealistic comparisons, and harmful judgments—and it will affect you at a subconscious level, so you won't even realize it is happening.

But it doesn't have to happen this way—you have the power to take back control.

You see, awareness changes everything. Awareness is your weapon against the hidden influences and damaging behaviors. While you are online, your mind, your thoughts, your core values are gravitating to wherever tech companies want you to go. The remedy is to limit the time you spend drifting in the online world and anchor yourself in real life—in real people and real conversations, in furry animals, interesting books, good music, and calming scenery, in cooking, photography, painting, and moving your body.

When your worth is in question, when you feel lost and alone, when you feel sad and can't explain why, anchor yourself in what centers you, makes you feel safe, and gives you hope.

I am with you.

I love you.

After empowering Natalie with this perspective, I suggested she order an alarm clock for her bedroom rather than use her phone to wake up for school. I was surprised there was no push-back when we talked about limiting phone use to a designated time after school and then a little more time after nightly swim team practice. She was also receptive when I asked her to start charging her phone in a separate area of the house until morning.

Almost instantly, I saw a difference. I noticed she was more present in main areas of the house, accepting invitations to play board games and help with the cooking. Her disposition was more cheerful, relaxed, and fun-loving. She began taking walks outside, often inviting me to go along. She was getting homework and household chores completed more efficiently.

It became routine for Natalie to charge her phone in my bathroom at night. Although her facial expression indicated this was something she'd never enjoy doing, her actions indicated she appreciated the reason why. Sometimes she'd plug in her phone, then crawl into my bed and take my hand.

Whenever Natalie did this, I felt a strong sense that her Grandpa Ben, Scott's father, was looking after us. Our family had gone to see him soon after his cancer diagnosis in 2017, not knowing that would be his final weekend on earth.

We'd spent the whole glorious weekend looking through his keepsake boxes and hearing his favorite life memories. Although Ben was in considerable pain, he continually grabbed my hand and squeezed it tightly.

Tether yourself, his action seemed to say, because in the end, our human connections, our relationships, our love for one another will be the only things that really matter.

> *Tether yourself, I say . . .*
> *So you don't drift away from what truly matters,*
> *So you don't forget your worth*
> *So you don't miss the moments that make life worth living.*
> *Tether yourself.*
> *It's what we must do for ourselves.*
> *It's what we must do for our children.*
> *It's what we must do for each other.*

I doubt many people would knowingly pick up a device that has been proven to negatively influence our thoughts, our choices, our actions, and our future happiness. Yet people who struggle with digital addiction face this choice every day. The virtual world created by social media and online gaming platforms provides an escape from reality and can have addictive qualities.

But awareness changes everything.

When we release what controls us, we are free to choose what matters most.

Let's choose what matters most.

Our lives are far too valuable to let drift away.

MAKING "NO TRADE" DECLARATIONS

Let's face it: when we choose to show up fully in the meaningful moments of life, we are making a trade. While it is not always possible to trade productivity and efficiency for human connection or inner peace, it is always worthwhile when we can.

One strategy that can increase our chances of making good trades while also providing positive modeling and support for our kids is making "no trade" declarations. Let me explain.

A few days after my father-in-law passed away, Scott and I were walking side-by-side on a busy downtown street. We had no destination in mind. We were walking in an effort to process the painful turn of events that had happened so quickly and unexpectedly.

At one point, Scott stopped right in the middle of the sidewalk, paying no mind to the people and cars rushing past, and made a declaration.

"I want to have more fun," he announced, taking my hands in his.

I can still smell the spring air, the exhaust of the cars, the storm brewing off in the distance. I don't think I will ever forget those words or the yearning they stirred up in me. I desperately wanted to have more fun, too, but how? What does that even look like in a life of non-negotiable duties, responsibilities, and obligations?

It took me only a few days to figure it out, and it came down to the trades I was *not* willing to make in my life. This was my declaration:

I'm not trading a conversation with my daughter for a mindless scroll on Instagram.

I'm not trading a proper hug and kiss goodbye for a rapid text response.

I'm not trading real human connection for shallow online friendships.

I'm not trading the experience of live music for a video clip.

I'm not trading a sunset's magnificent descent for a cleverly captioned photo.

I'm not trading the joy of a handwritten card for a generic birthday message on a good friend's news feed.

I'm not trading Likes for real love.

I'm not trading rest for 24/7 availability.

I'm not trading my purpose for promotion.

I'm not trading the feeling of someone's hand in mine for the temporary satisfaction of an empty inbox.

Perhaps you'd like to make some "no trade" declarations of your own.

Take a moment to think about how your work, your technology, and your life might bleed into each other to the point that there are no longer any protected areas. For many people, daily distraction is routinely invited into sacred spaces of life—the bedroom, family meals, vacations, even during the middle of the night when sleep should be the priority. By making a family commitment to designated screen-free times and a home base for devices, we are able to make good trades without sacrificing our responsibilities and obligations.

Having protected times and spaces also supports our kids in their need for downtime away from the pressures and expectations of the online world. Anya Kamenetz, author of *The Art of Screen Time*, has found that many teens admit they appreciate these prescribed breaks.[2]

I found it quite interesting that I only had to mention once to my daughter that I feel lonely when she is on her phone while I'm driving; from that point on, she's kept her phone in her backpack, and we now have some of the most enjoyable talks while we're in the car.

By creating daily non-screen rituals—such as walking the dog without the phone, making meals using cookbooks instead of phones, and having uninterrupted Talk Time with the young person in your life—you provide the human connection that is often lacking in the lives of teens (both online and in real life). Plus, it's incredibly motivating to think that someday, the young person in your life will remember you holding a leash, a book, a fishing pole, or their hand instead of a phone.

As our family learned in the most painful way, there's no way to know how much time we have left with our loved ones. Let's find peace in knowing we're making good trades, the best kind of trades—the kind of trades that feel like we're finishing the game with the best possible hand, stacked with *relationships, memories, purpose,* and *love.*

It's easy to justify burying our heads in a phone to answer a text from a friend, research the factual nature of something you heard, or garner a good laugh at a funny video, but I can assure you that in our final days, those aren't the memories we will hold dear. Instead, we will reflect on experiences, adventures, and interactions with our friends and loved ones.

---

2. Anya Kamenetz, qtd. in Leah Shafer, "Social Media and Teen Anxiety," *Usable Knowledge* (blog), *Harvard Graduate School of Education*, December 15, 2017, https://www.gse.harvard.edu/news/uk/17/12/social-media-and-teen-anxiety.

ANCHORING THROUGH INVITATION

During my highly distracted years, I got defensive when Scott brought it to my attention that I was spending too much time on tech and drifting from what mattered most. In the face of even the gentlest reminder, I became irrational and immediately shut him out. When I look back now, I recognize that type of behavior was a red flag, a warning that technology had taken an unprecedented and unhealthy priority in my life.

As my self-awareness and healthy digital boundaries have grown, *I* am now the one who brings excessive tech use to my own attention. And when I notice I'm spending too much time on my device and/or using it as an escape or a barrier, I don't hide my relapse in shame. Instead, I acknowledge it and face it honestly in order to gain support and accountability from my loved ones.

I'm convinced we must do this for ourselves, for each other, and for our kids.

As I was attempting to draft a manuscript for my first-ever children's book one fall, I had to call myself out. I was having difficulty focusing for even short periods of time as the need to monitor social media and respond quickly to messages had become all-encompassing. By constantly starting and stopping my writing process, I couldn't gain momentum. I quickly realized it was going to take me years to write a six-hundred-word children's book if I didn't find my focus! While this experience was extremely frustrating, it was also very eye-opening. It gave me greater compassion and understanding for what many of our kids experience on a daily basis.

I began searching for an anchor quote—powerful words I could read whenever I began drifting—that would immediately bring me back to center. The moment I read this quote by Charles D. Gill, I knew I'd found my anchor:

"There are many wonderful things that will never be done if you do not do them."

After reading it several times, I noticed I was crying—not for myself, but for every young person who will never fulfill his or her purpose, never know true inner peace, never have the ability to be fully present in the moment because of digital distraction.

There is a reason Silicon Valley executives do not give their children iPads and set screen-time limits on digital devices. They know the risks and dangers, but most notably, they know the cost.

Not fulfilling our purpose because we're wasting our time and attention Snapchatting, texting, posting, tracking Likes and shares, and mindlessly scrolling our lives away could very well be the greatest cost of technology to human life.

And there I was, succumbing to its elusiveness once again.

I refused to get sucked back in and let its allure control me.

I immediately handwrote my anchor quote on a small slip of paper and decided on three *wonderful things* I'd set out to do that very day. My *wonderful things* fell neatly into three categories: making human connections, reaching my dreams, and practicing self-care.

Next to the quote, I drew a clock and used a brightly colored highlighter to mark the specific blocks of time I was committing to these activities without interruption—these were the promises I was making to myself. I then set the little slip where I would see it throughout the day.

Using this awareness and accountability strategy each morning for five days, I was astounded by what I accomplished. I finished writing the manuscript for the children's book. I prepared a PowerPoint presentation for an upcoming speaking event. I attended a group exercise class that I'd been both too scared and too busy to try for months. I delivered flowers and a copy of my book *Only Love Today* to an elderly neighbor I'd been meaning to visit for over a year. I sent seven cards to people who'd been on my mind and in my heart.

It appeared I'd found an antidote for the lure of digital distraction:

Having a purpose
backed by a promise
is stronger than anything that distracts us from it.

I decided it would be tragic not to share my discovery with the person in my life who probably needed it most: my teenage daughter. But when I excitedly showed Natalie my collection of promise slips, I got a less than enthusiastic response.

"You're not going to ask me to do that, are you?" Natalie asked, looking at the papers like they were a pile of rotten bananas.

I asked her to hear me out. She scooted over so there was room for me on her bed. I then shared how the online world had been impacting my productivity and briefly described two correlating studies that provided relevant information:

- Merely having your phone on your desk or in your bag next to you is enough to decrease your brainpower. (This happens even when you can't see your phone.) Those who kept their phones in the other room did better on tasks than those who kept their phones on their desks or in their bags or pockets.[3]
- The unexpected interruptions caused by the phone have a huge impact on your productivity. It takes an average of twenty-three minutes and fifteen seconds to get back to the task after you've been interrupted, and you never actually get back to the level of focus you had pre-interruption.[4]

---

3. Amanda Chan, "Having Your Phone on Your Desk or in Your Bag Can Affect Brainpower, Study Shows," *Teen Vogue*, August 2, 2017, https://www.teenvogue.com/story/phone-brainpower-cognitive-effect-desk-bag-pocket.

4. Kristin Wong, "How Long It Takes to Get Back on Track after a Distraction," *Lifehacker* (blog), July 29, 2017, https://lifehacker.com/how-long-it-takes-to-get-back-on-track-after-a-distract-1720708353.

Unlike the Tethering Talk she and I had approximately six months prior, Natalie did not seem interested in what I was sharing. I decided to be completely honest with her about my deepest concern.

"There are many kids in your school who are going to get to the end of their senior year and realize the time they spent on their phone cost them a chance to do what they most want to do in life, and that makes me really sad," I said.

Natalie released an audible sigh, which led me to believe she was done with our conversation.

I was wrong; it was only getting started.

What came next was an unexpected barrage of emotion and fear.

It would have been easy to meet my child's emotions with my own or to throw down ultimatums, but I remembered how I'd felt years before when Scott offered me much-needed awareness into my own addictive patterns with technology.

Embracing my role as an empathic Encourager, I remained seated and listening, and I reminded my daughter how much I care about her mind, body, heart, and future.

When we got through the intense emotions and heated push-back, what was left hanging between us was a brave and honest question she'd asked: "But what else can I do?"

Natalie's question uncovered an enlightening truth: we are raising a generation of kids who do not remember a time before the internet. We are raising a generation of kids whose lives are embedded in technology. It should come as no surprise, then, that many of them don't know what to do with their downtime.

I was quick to offer up some ideas, mentioning several fulfilling, real-life alternatives to the soul-depleting online world. When she didn't respond, I remembered—what is far more powerful than throwing out ideas? Extending an invitation.

"You know, accomplishing small tasks that we set out to do,

like baking cookies, taking a walk, or planting flowers creates a sense of accomplishment that builds confidence and motivation to tackle bigger and harder tasks," I said. "I was about to do some spring cleaning in the pantry. You are so good at organizing. Would you come join me? I'd love to have your help."

Natalie's head tilted to the side. I could tell she was considering it.

"I'll give you a few minutes to think about it," I said, remembering how my former high school students tended to make good decisions when they were given the space and freedom to do so.

As I began pulling items off the shelves, I remembered how uplifting it felt as a teen to organize my closet and rearrange my room. Seeing tangible and immediate results brought a sense of accomplishment to my insecure fifteen-year-old heart. It felt so satisfying to get things in order when my life felt like a mess. It was greatly comforting to do something mindless when adolescent pressure and drama constantly inhabited my brain.

I heard Natalie come into the kitchen. Scott, not knowing I had invited her to help me, asked her to join him in shucking some corn. At first, there was resistance, but as Scott began telling Natalie a story about his grandpa's farm, the tension eased, and laughter filled the kitchen.

Pretty soon, there she was, offering to help me organize. Natalie quickly noticed that the cats' feeding room (a.k.a. the coat closet) needed a good cleaning and better organization. An hour later, there was a glowing floor, cat food cans were organized by flavor, water bowls were freshly filled, and a carefree smile had returned to my daughter's face.

As my girl stood at the door of the closet admiring her handywork, she said, "Do you want to take a walk after dinner, Mom?"

There was no way I was going to pass up that invitation.

I'm convinced this is what we must do for each other:

We must invite each other into the messy spaces of our lives—

the ones we don't want to show anyone, the ones no one sees on social media. We must invite each other to have hard conversations and be willing to sit and listen as emotions come spilling out. We must not stay closed up, separated, disconnected, unfulfilled, and adrift. We must extend our hands and find each other in the middle of the mess.

Our kids will live under our roof for only a short while, but their childhood experiences will have a lasting impact on their lives.

Perhaps when they have homes and lives of their own, it will be a cob of corn or a closet in need of cleaning that will take them back to a moment in time when we invited them into the messy, yet sacred spaces of life.

Let nothing distract us from doing the most *wonderful thing* we are here to do: *live.*

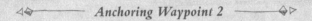

Anchoring Waypoint 2

INVITING KIDS TO CULTIVATE MINDFUL TECH USAGE

While it is necessary to help our kids set limits on technology, empowering them to manage boundaries and exercise moderation is paramount. Here are several ideas for helping young people begin to hold themselves accountable for their media consumption—behaviors that will have lifelong benefits.

Identify "red flag behaviors" so kids learn to listen to their body's need for a break. Early on in my Hands-Free journey, I identified "red flag behaviors" regarding my tech use. I defined them as behaviors that interfered with my ability to connect to what truly mattered in life.

- Feeling panicky if you don't have the phone
- Feeling the need to check the device compulsively
- Reaching for the phone during conversations, during wait times, or in situations where it is dangerous to do so, such as at stop lights and while driving
- Overreacting or becoming irritated when someone speaks to you while you are on your device
- Picking up the phone first thing upon waking rather than taking time to set intentions based on the priorities of one's heart
- Feeling as if you need to respond immediately to messages
- Feeling inadequate, sad, or inferior as a result of the images or posts you are seeing

I make it a point to talk with my kids about these warning signs regularly.

As you discuss your own red flag behaviors, ask your kids what feelings they notice when they are on tech devices too long. Together, plan some good options for "tethering" themselves instead to real-life experiences or small projects that create a sense of accomplishment.

Point out that social media does not often portray the whole and accurate view of someone's life. I have made many mistakes when it comes to technology, but I knew I'd done one thing well when Natalie gave a dieting friend some healthy perspective about the models and celebrities they see in the media. When I commended her on the advice she gave her friend, she offered me additional examples of kids she knew in real life who were portraying their lives as "perfect," when the reality was far from it. She mentioned how aware she is that everyone has struggles and people only post their highlights. This awareness decreases the tendency to compare and conclude she is "less than."

Not only is it critical for young people to understand that the images they see are often hand selected, posed, and filtered, but they also need to understand they have a choice about who they allow to come into their lives and influence them. Encouraging kids to be selective and not only follow positive, beneficial accounts, but also to create them is a great way to help them pay attention to the power comparison can have in their lives.

Manage time collaboratively. When a member of my Soul Shift online course expressed concern about her son's gaming habits, I reached out to Kerry Foreman, a licensed psychotherapist who runs teen groups on tech mindfulness and has a son who is an avid gamer. Kerry's advice was this:

> We can empower our teens by helping them time manage—which requires collaboration, not correction. What limits would your son put on himself if he could choose? What limits do parents want? Meet in the middle somewhere. Most adults spend more than two hours a day in front of a screen, so they may want to ask themselves what they are modeling. Are they willing to scale back?
>
> If the teen is doing well in school, the parent can reward his good choices by assuming he will time manage in this area. If he doesn't, they can cross that bridge when they come to it, but don't assume he will make the wrong choices when his general behavior pattern shows otherwise.

Kerry went on to say that her teenage son manages his own gaming time and does so more effectively than when she and her partner were enforcing limits. Her son enjoys the empowerment that comes from showing his parents he's capable in that area.

It is important to note that kids who are involved with developing the plan for screen usage are more likely to follow the rules they helped create. Building consensus is important for buy-in and trust building.

Build momentum in non-screen activities. One of the most intriguing blog posts about empowering kids to cultivate healthy technology use and non-screen hobbies is titled, "How I Limited Screen Time by Offering My Kids Unlimited Screen Time." The concept is based on personal momentum. As a freelance writer, the author of the post, known only as The Narrowback Slacker, finds that if she begins her day in a productive manner, it's likely she will continue to be productive throughout the day. She found this to be true for her kids as well. So she came up with a unique solution she calls the "Momentum Optimization Project," or "The List," which is an agenda of tasks her children must accomplish each day before they have unlimited screen time. It reads:

Absolutely no glowing screens until:

- You have read real text (not comics) for at least 25 minutes
- All your homework is done (one item may wait until morning with approval from Mom/Dad)
- You have marked the calendar with any upcoming tests or deadlines and made an appointment to study with Mom/Dad
- You have done something creative, active, or productive for at least 45 minutes
- Your bed is made, and your room is tidy
- You have done at least one chore[5]

5. Narrowback Slacker, "How I Limited Screen Time by Offering My Kids Unlimited Screen Time," May 14, 2014, *Narrowback Slacker* (blog), https://narrowbackslacker.com/2014/05/13/how-i-limited-screen-time-by-offering-my-kids-unlimited-screen-time/.

The author's goal wasn't to make the kids not play on the computer or not watch TV. It was to remind them that there are other ways to spend their time, too.

Embrace built-in tools to help curb usage. I was overjoyed when Apple provided iPhone/iPad users with a tool for boundary setting called "Screen Time." Scott and I immediately knew we wanted to implement it on our devices, as well as on our daughters' devices. Naturally, our kids were resistant to the idea. To be honest, even I was a bit hesitant. Did I really want to know how much time I spent on my device and how many times I picked it up each hour? And did I really want my phone to go dark once I reached my limit? But as soon as our family began receiving this information, one question became clear: *Is this really how I want to spend X minutes or hours a day?* With awareness comes discernment, and we all began to make better choices in how we were using our time, focus, and energy. Not only did work habits and creativity surge, but there was more connection, conversation, laughter, and togetherness.

None of us have parented in the digital age, so let's decide in advance to accept all the help we can get. We have the power and the responsibility to continually reach for our kids and bring them back to real experiences, honest conversations, quiet moments, and things that ground them. If we need help and support in doing that, let's bravely share our challenges and ask for that help and support. If we've found a solution that works in our household or classroom, let's share it boldly in hopes that it might empower others. The vast network the internet provides isn't all negative; we now have resources and support at our fingertips to become better informed and connect with others in similar situations. Like most good things, respect for its power and moderation are keys to living well in this digital age.

ANCHORING THROUGH PROTECTION

When the guide asked which of us would like to be in front of the kayak, Natalie volunteered eagerly. This echoed my current experience—her stepping forth, taking the lead, sometimes looking back at me and sometimes not.

But within two minutes of sitting down inside that kayak, I knew booking this excursion during my daughters' spring break was one of the best decisions I'd ever made.

Sounds dramatic.

Sounds over-the-top.

But at the time—as it so often does nowadays—I felt like our family needed a tranquil escape, undisturbed and unmarred by noise, distraction, societal influence, and pressure.

Scott and Avery were in one boat, Natalie and I in another. As we glided out of the South Carolina marina, the peace settling onto our faces was unmistakable. Life had been especially heavy with the unexpected loss of Scott's father. But on the water, things instantly felt lighter.

"Mama, look over there." Natalie pointed excitedly to a flock of herons.

She'd called me Mama, I noted. Somewhere along the line, I'd become more maturely addressed as "Mom." I cherish the occasional "Mama" that slips out.

Natalie and I worked together to maneuver the kayak. We laughed when we steered incorrectly and began going backwards. Once we got into a rhythm, she described what she'd learned in science about bird migration and coastal ecosystems. I rejoiced in her atypical chatter.

When Natalie became quiet, I studied the back of her head. Two almost-even braids she'd made herself rested against her life jacket. I'd grown so used to seeing her hair in carefully curled waves; the crooked braids reminded me that my baby was still there, snapped into a bright orange vest that hugged her petite body.

Oh, how I want to keep her safe.

My eyes spotted beautiful homes backing up to the marsh. What were the current worries of the people who lived there, I wondered? Did they shop for bathing suits with their daughters and wonder why they had so little fabric? Did they worry about their kids texting explicit pictures to one another, only to have them airdropped into the world for perpetuity? Did they struggle with concerns about the overload of homework that's keeping young brains up past midnight and increasing the risk of depression and risky behavior?

Stop. Just stop, I told my brain-that-never-quits.

Moments like this are rare jewels, I reminded myself. I had my daughter's full attention, and she had mine.

If I could live anywhere, it would be here, I thought—a salt marsh in South Carolina where one can hear the oysters spitting and the wind blowing through the cord grass.

I didn't want to live here so much for me, but for my daughter . . . and her younger sister . . . and for their friends and all the kids who have the world at their fingertips—kids whose view of themselves and of life is skewed by information, images, opinions, and pressures from a glowing screen.

I want to keep them tethered to something real.

That was my wish as I turned my attention to the setting sun and recited a prayer of gratitude for this moment and an appeal for divine guidance for Scott and me as we steer our children through life.

Regrettably, the guide informed us we had to return to land before the sun set completely. Our legs shaky from boating, we laughed and hopped on our bikes to head back to our vacation rental, quickly realizing the bike path was not well-lit.

"I have an idea," Scott called out.

He turned on the flashlight of his phone and put it in the bicycle basket, creating a headlight. He had me do the same with my phone.

Our family biked back to our rental—him in the lead, me in the back, our phone lights illuminating the path and our most precious gifts in between.

I want to keep them tethered to love.

It was a common theme that week of spring vacation.

Several weeks later, Avery was writing a persuasive essay about why she needed a phone. I knew it was not the right time, nor was it necessary for her to have one, but I was interested in hearing her reasoning.

Reason five gave me chills: "I could use my phone as a light like Dad did if I am ever in trouble, lost, kidnapped, or without power. The phone could light my way home."

I realized this was preteen logic and an attempt to convince me to say yes because of my desire for her to be safe. Still, it made me think that the experience we'd shared riding home in the dark had been more than just a bike ride. For her, it had been a teachable moment underscoring a child's greatest need. Should she find herself in darkness one day, the thing she'd want most would be to find her way back home.

I found it no coincidence that her older sister came to me, wanting to watch a controversial show marketed to teens that graphically portrayed suicide. I told her my concerns, which echoed those expressed by mental health professionals. Natalie listened to my reasoning but didn't quite seem convinced.

"You were right," she said later in a follow-up conversation. "I talked to my friend, and she said the same things you did. She started to watch the first episode but turned it off. It messed with her mind. I don't want to watch it after all."

Before she turned to go, Natalie said, "I'd come to you before I'd ever hurt myself." And with those assuring words, I had an *aha* moment.

As parents, we desperately want to protect our children's physical, emotional, mental, and spiritual well-being—but maybe it's not about *keeping* them safe; maybe it's about *loving* them safe.

Protecting kids from the dangers and pressures of the outside world does not come from empty threats or good intentions; it comes from experiencing life together, from being in the same boat. It comes when we make ourselves available to listen, learn how to recalibrate the course after taking wrong turns, and share some laughter and sunsets along the way.

To put it simply, our children's future protection is instilled through the loving actions of today.

Confirmation of this belief came in a powerful article written by licensed psychotherapist Heather DiDomenico. Greeting me in big, bold letters when I clicked on the link was this sentence: "The more you show love to your children, the bigger their brains grow." Dr. DiDomenico explained:

> The truth is that the more you show love to your children with a hug, a kiss, a smile, unconditional positive regard, by including them, being interested in them, through family-based play, and so much more of the nurturing type of communication, the bigger their brains grow.
>
> Beyond the basic human needs of food, water, and housing, love and nurturing not only builds the pathway for our children's future happiness, but also survival. . . . The brain's ability to grow in response to love can be seen as a way to keep humans banded together against danger and intruders.[6]

Equally encouraging was a research study that concluded it is not too late for warm, supportive parents to make a difference. According to a 2015 study published in *Developmental Cognitive Neuroscience*, teens who grew closer to their parents starting at age fifteen showed less activation of a brain region linked to risk-taking

---

6. Heather DiDomenico, "Psychologist Reveals What Makes Kids' Brains Grow Bigger," *Lifehack* (blog), January 28, 2016, https://www.lifehack.org/356753/psychologist-says-what-kids-think-about-love-reflects-how-they-think.

and took fewer chances eighteen months later. Because adolescents are more apt than children to engage in risky behaviors (such as reckless driving, substance use, and unprotected sexual activity), it is crucial to examine what protective factors decrease the negative behaviors that lead to these potentially life-altering circumstances. Increased closeness between parent and teen (which includes having parents' respect and help talking through problems, and an absence of arguing or yelling) is one such factor.

Given this hopeful information, I created a mnemonic using the word "protection" to help remind Encouragers of the specific loving practices that bolster our kids' overall well-being:

P—Positive feedback and touch
R—Responsiveness
O—Open-ended questions
T—Time
E—Empathy
C—Connection
T—Trust
I—Independence
O—Opportunities
N—Notice and nurture

In the weeks that remained between spring break and the conclusion of the school year, Avery began packing her lunch the night before school. Practicing the protective components of "opportunities" and "independence" from the list above, I stepped back and let her do it for herself.

One night, I watched as she extracted a pack of *Only Love Today* lunch notes from the kitchen drawer. The pocket-sized cards contained favorite soul-building phrases that I used throughout my teaching years. Although I designed them with the intention that someone would choose a card to give to someone else,

I stayed quiet as Avery selected one for herself. Out of all twenty-five cards, Avery picked up the card that said, *I learn a lot from you.*

Interestingly, she was the inspiration behind that phrase when I designed the cards.

"Can I put this one in my lunch box?" Avery asked.

"Yes, absolutely," I said, detecting a deeper meaning behind the choice.

Avery's brain knew that message was for her. I've said it to her many times. She knew this inherently, and I believe it's why she reached for that card.

Avery placed the card inside her lunchbox, put it in the fridge, and set her backpack by the door.

"I'm ready to face the world tomorrow!" she said confidently.

And although we were not floating in a secluded marsh tucked safely away from the world, life felt lighter; the future looked less scary.

"You *are* ready," I agreed and opened my arms, knowing this simple action held great power.

Love has a way of reminding us what we know deep down, and that is what will help us survive in this tricky world.

I am learning.

She is learning.

We are in the boat together.

And love will expand our minds, along with our hearts, propelling us safely forward toward the promise of a new day.

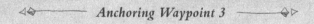
Anchoring Waypoint 3

WORDS THAT CAN'T WAIT

I will not soon forget the words in a letter written by a middle schooler who bravely admitted he or she could not stop thinking about suicide. The school had received the letter from an anonymous email address, and because they could not track the sender, they posted it to the entire school community, hoping someone might recognize their child in the words.

Two lines stuck out to me:

"I can't tell my parents," and, "I really need someone to talk to."

A reader whose child was part of the school system had reached out to me for help because she thought of me as someone who "knows what to say to hurting children." She asked me to draft a message she could send in reply to the anonymous email address.

Although I provided her with encouragements and information for the student in need, I couldn't stop thinking about the young person's words and knew I needed to do more. I began spreading this important message through my online community: We cannot assume our kids know we are a safe haven; we must *tell* them; we must *show* them.

Using the feedback I've received from young people through the Index Card Exercise, I prepared the following script for adults. These are the words a young person who feels desperately alone and unloved needs to hear today:

> *Hey, can I sit with you for a minute? I'm not great at expressing myself, so I ask that you bear with me for a moment while I tell you a few important things.*
>
> *I know that sometimes it must feel like I am always on you, asking you if you've gotten things done, pushing you to do well. I do that because I want you to have the best possible life you can have. But lately, I realized I need to remember that today is the most important day to focus*

on. *And who you are right now, at this very moment, is someone I am very proud of.*

I don't say it enough, but you amaze me. You amaze me with your talents, your humor, your smarts, your heart, your energy, your courage, your determination.

You amaze me by the way you handle the pressures and challenges of school, extracurricular activities, friend-ships, growing up, and taking care of yourself.

You amaze me by the way you keep trying, no matter what comes at you.

Growing up in today's world includes challenges that I didn't have, and sometimes it's hard for me to fully grasp what it must be like for you. But lately, I've been trying to put myself in your shoes and imagine what it must be like to handle it all.

One thing I am certain of is how hard the school years can be on a person's spirit. These years can seem endless and hopeless at times. But you have the strength and the resilience to get through them. Just keep taking it day by day, and before you know it, there will be a great, big world waiting for you. I can already see you as an adult, doing something fulfilling with your many gifts that will contribute to this community and have an impact in this world.

I don't say it enough, but I see beyond the grades, the effort, and the outer shell to who you are becoming. I see someone really incredible in you.

Please know I don't expect you to be perfect, and it's okay to make mistakes as you grow and learn—I know I sure did. There is no mistake bigger than my love for you. There is nothing we can't get through together.

One last thing. I know that sometimes it is hard to say things in person, so here is a notebook I want you to use to talk to me. Take your pain, your worries, your problems, and your fears, and put them on the pages. Put it under my pillow when you have something you want me to know. Your notes will help me know how I can be the parent you need me to be. I will not judge the words and thoughts you share with me. I will listen and learn from you.

I went ahead and started the journal.

These may look like words, but they are more than words. These are lifelines for tough times. Please remember these truths:

No mistake you make is bigger than my love for you.

You are never alone.

I love you, just as you are today.

Although it's difficult to imagine our own child could be the one hurting so badly, we must consider it. In the school system where the troubled student resides, many people acknowledged it could be their child, and there was an outpouring of affirming messages sent to the anonymous email address. While the outcome of this particular student's situation is unknown, the community was forever changed by this young person's courage and were inspired to connect with their kids in ways they hadn't before.

Let us remember that every young person needs connection today, no matter what happened in the past . . . no matter how unresponsive your child is. . . . no matter how awkward it feels to say the words. Please say them. *Connection is key because listening is love.* Let no child feel alone in his or her darkest hour.

LIVE LOVE NOW REFLECTION: IF WISHES BECOME INVITATIONS

My greatest wishes for my firstborn daughter when she was a baby included being anything she wanted to be and living a happy, prosperous life. While those wishes are still valid, they shifted to far less grandiose ones around the time she turned ten. My wish became this: *I want her to live . . . I want her to experience life with all her senses . . . I want her to experience life in living color, face-to-face, with two open hands.* For my child who is growing up in a text-happy, vitamin D-deficient, connection-hungry culture, I came to have simple—yet increasingly rare—life-enhancing wishes.

My Wish for You: A Living Life

I wish you crickets that lull you to sleep.
I wish you pumpkin guts oozing through your fingers.
I wish you the most perfect s'mores stick you can find.
I wish you the ability to be alone with your thoughts.

I wish you the feeling of someone's hand in your back pocket.
I wish you shade from a Weeping Willow tree.
I wish you goodbye kisses and puppy dog fur.
I wish you moments of complete silence.

I wish you freshly squeezed lemonade made by your hands.
*I wish you spontaneous gatherings where no one wants to leave
    the table.*
I wish you porch swings and bare feet.
I wish you sea breezes.

I wish you a deck of playing cards that slide from your fingers.
I wish you historic monuments and sunsets that make you feel small.
I wish you books in bed.
I wish you peace.

I wish you answers without Google.
I wish you mindless wandering with a good old-fashioned map.
I wish you boredom that leads to the best ideas you've ever had.
I wish you starry nights.

I wish you people watching from the city bus window.
I wish you talented street musicians who make you stop and stare.
I wish you flowers from Pike Place Market that burst with color.
I wish you joy.

I wish you laughter from a small child that makes you look up.
I wish you wrinkled hands to embrace you and share stories of
   long ago.
I wish you handwritten notes in your mailbox.
I wish you a chance to heal a broken soul.

I wish you memories and someone who holds the door for you.
I wish you smiles that are not for public consumption.
I wish you travels without fear and safety worries.
I wish you inner peace.

I wasn't quite finished with my list; I felt there were more to be written, but the unwritten lines would have to wait. In the midst of my writing, my brown-eyed girl asked me if we could go to "Rock River." I started taking my daughters there when I was writing my second book, when deadlines and productivity threatened my health and well-being. "Rock River," as we all began to call it, was my refuge, my place of peace, and I always brought my kids along.

"But this time, Mama," Natalie said, "I want to invite my friend."

I was surprised. It was usually just us.

"She's been looking really sad," ten-year-old Natalie explained. "I've asked her what is wrong, but she's not ready to talk about it. I thought maybe going to the river would help. It is so peaceful there. I always feel better after I collect rocks."

As I looked into her humongous eyes that held so much hope, I felt as if one of my wishes had just come true. Perhaps I didn't need to keep adding to the list after all. With great relief, I realized that life experiences do not have to diminish with each new version of the iPhone. Human connection does not have to weaken as the need for Wi-Fi grows. The electronic screen does not have to become a substitute for life's richest experiences—not if we pass down the tradition to live.

A young person can inherit my love for baking if I invite her into the kitchen.

A young person can inherit my need for walking outdoors if I ask her to join me.

A young person can inherit my thirst for authentic conversation if I open up and give her time to talk.

A young person can inherit my love for music if I take her to concerts and listen to what she likes.

A young person can inherit my places of refuge if I take her to wade in the river.

A young person can inherit life's richest experiences if wishes become invitations.

So let us keep wishing—it'll keep us intentional.

Let us keep living—it'll keep us alive.

Let us keep inviting—it'll keep our precious children from drifting off course.

REFLECTION QUESTIONS

1. How dependent are you on technology? For example, how quickly do you look at your phone when you wake up in the morning? Is it difficult to then put the phone down? Is technology part of your bedtime or mealtime routine?

Do you ever do things in your spare time without your phone? Do you routinely turn off your phone? In what ways has technology dependence negatively impacted your life, your health, or your relationships?

2. What is one change you would like to make around technology, and what steps will you take to do so?

3. How often do you talk to the young people you love about their digital lives? Do you feel you could know more about what apps, websites, and games they are into? Do you feel like they could benefit from more talks about how to navigate the online world? If so, how might you go about it? What might you say?

4. What worries you most about your own technology consumption? About your child's technology consumption? What actions or conversations might you have to address that concern?

5. How might you be more of an Encourager rather than an enforcer in respect to your kids' technology use? What might be some benefits of adopting that role?

6. Do you feel satisfied with the number of non-screen activities you do with the young people in your life each week or month? What steps might you take to increase those experiences? How might you involve the young people in your life in planning those activities and experiences?

CHAPTER 4

MICROMANAGED

> *There are only two lasting bequests we can hope to give*
> *our children. One of these is roots, the other, wings.*
>
> —Hodding Carter, *Where Main*
> *Street Meets the River*

Several years ago, after an especially chaotic rush out the door
to go on a family vacation, I sat in the passenger seat fuming—
fuming because I didn't have time to put the dishes in the dish-
washer, fuming because we were late getting on the road, fuming
because the garage door was acting up, fuming because things
were not going according to plan—*my plan*—the one everybody
in my family was subjected to, whether they liked it or not.

That's when Scott turned to me with the most somber expression and said, "You're never happy anymore."

I wanted to defend.

I wanted to excuse.

I wanted to deny.

I wanted to say, *"What on earth do you mean?"*

But I couldn't say anything. I just sat there in silence because
I knew Scott was right.

I couldn't quite pinpoint when I'd changed from a positive, agreeable person to a negative, controlling one; I only knew that I had. I secretly reminisced about the hopeful special education teacher I once was—the one who saw the good in her students and patiently prepared them to accomplish tasks and goals no one thought they could ever manage on their own.

Looking back, I realized I was doing all the things I encouraged the parents of my former students *not* to do.

I continually rushed in; I had all the answers; I knew the best way to do everything; I could do things faster and more efficiently, so I took over. And anything my children *did* do for themselves was never up to my standards. Rather than raising my kids to be self-sufficient, self-motivated, and self-assured, I micromanaged them until there was no room to breathe, grow, or thrive.

My entrepreneurial, dream-pursuing older daughter's desire to initiate several projects at once, try every recipe in the cookbook, and leave messy trails in her wake received disapproving looks on a daily basis.

My stop-and-smell-the-roses younger daughter's desire to carefully accessorize every part of her body before we left the house, buckle in her stuffed animals before we put the car in drive, and examine every insect along our path drew harsh prodding more often than not.

My children needed an encouraging parent who allowed them to discover their strengths and their purpose through trial and error, but what they had was a critical manager with an agenda focused on efficiency, perfection, and control.

I am ashamed to admit that I treated my own children so differently from the way I'd treated my students. In my distracted, depleted, and inauthentic state, my life felt chaotic. I was willing to do just about anything to maintain a sense of control—even if it meant depriving my kids of the opportunity to complete age-appropriate tasks, make age-appropriate decisions, and build self-confidence while doing so.

Forget about living. Forget about smiling. Forget about experiencing gratitude, peace, or fulfillment. When you base your happiness on tasks being completed, plans running accordingly, and a certain image being portrayed, you're just setting yourself up for disappointment. No wonder I'd lost my joy.

Mornings were especially chaotic at my house, sending my micromanaging tendencies into overdrive. Hair brushing was a task my young daughters were fully capable of doing themselves, yet I insisted on doing it for them to "save time." Each morning, Natalie obediently stood still while I hastily brushed her hair, pretending not to see her wince in pain. We were in a rush, after all; I hated to be late.

When it was Avery's turn, she'd almost always ask if she could brush her own hair. My response alternated between, "We don't have time today," and "When you get a little bigger."

On this particular morning, my then-four-year-old child did not ask if she could brush her own hair. I was relieved. I could do a quick ponytail, prod Avery to put on her shoes, and be out the door in less than two minutes, I calculated—because managers always calculate.

As I aggressively gathered Avery's unruly curls into my palm, I happened to get a glimpse of my reflection. My brows were knotted together tightly. My mouth was set in a hard, thin line. I looked haggard, hopeless, and sad. I would have dismissed this disturbing sight had it not been for Scott's painful words that had remained with me long after the vacation had ended.

"You're never happy anymore."

I felt my face grow hot. Tears began to pool, but I blinked them back—because managers know there's no time for tears. But instead of continuing to brush with vigor, I suddenly stopped. With trembling hands, I held out the hairbrush to my child.

"How would you do it?" I asked quietly.

At first, Avery looked shocked, as if I were offering her a hairy tarantula. But as I continued to hold out the brush, Avery eventually picked it up.

With small but agile hands, she stroked the sides of her hair from top to bottom until the hair was silky smooth. While lost in her joyful task, it appeared she forgot I was there. After a few minutes, she carefully brought the hair forward to drape softly over her shoulders. Then she smiled proudly at her reflection. The manager in me noticed she neglected to brush the back of her head, but I remained quiet.

My child met my eyes in the mirror's reflection. "Thank you, Mama. I always wanted to do that."

I prayed God would help me do something, anything, with those significant words she'd gifted to me.

For the next several weeks, we finished up breakfast a few minutes earlier so Avery could brush her own hair, and I could watch . . . and learn.

"Want me to show you how I do it?" Avery said each morning as I held out the brush.

I could not deny the look of contentment on Avery's face as a result of doing her own hair, in her own way. Seeing how this simple act created a major sense of accomplishment motivated me to continue stepping back. I felt hopeful that I could return to being the optimistic and affirming Encourager I'd been with my students. Although my pupils had severe behavioral and learning issues, I made a point to find at least one strength in each student on which to build. With firm but loving guidance and expectations, I gave my students the space and opportunity to try. They often made mistakes, some with pretty tough natural consequences, but I never faltered in my belief that my students could reach their individual goals.

Ironically, the biggest obstacles for many of my students were their parents. I often had to remind parents that by doing tasks their children could do for themselves, they were sending a clear message to their kids that they were not capable. I stressed the importance of letting go of the need to have things done exactly as they would do them (and on their timetable) in order to foster their child's independence. I also helped parents understand that shame and criticism were demotivating, but acceptance, belief, and validation served as fuel.

Heeding the very advice I once gave my students' parents and practicing the skills and vocabulary that made me an effective educator, the atmosphere in our home immediately changed.

Saying, "Take your time," a phrase from my teaching days, had a profound effect on Avery. This highly observant child, who had lived under constant pressure to hurry, was so encouraged by these three words, I began to use them liberally, as if I'd discovered a miraculous cure for a wound I hadn't even known I was inflicting. The way these words caused Avery's shoulders to lift and her smile to widen led me to declare them Soul-Building Words. "Take your time" ignited in her a desire to accomplish necessary tasks to the best of her ability and to take initiative to begin other tasks as well.

Parenting would be much simpler if we could apply the same remedies to each of our children, but that's just not the way it works, is it? With Natalie, my conscientious firstborn, I could see that a fear of failure had been holding her back from taking healthy risks. Knowing this fear was likely caused by my harsh reactions to her mistakes in the past, I began doing repair work. I used the "How would you do it?" question, which had worked so well with Avery, but with Natalie I followed it up with additional assurances: *It's natural to make mistakes when we're trying something new. Mistakes mean we're learning. I mess up sometimes, too.*

As I observed my children performing tasks and making decisions without assistance, I saw a critical connection between demonstrating responsibility and feeling valued—the type of unshakable value that comes from feeling needed, capable, appreciated, and part of something bigger than oneself. Not only did my daughters embrace the responsibility they so deeply craved, but they took it to the next level, revealing hidden strengths fueled by internal motivation. Once I saw my children begin to flourish, I knew it was time to resign as manager and embrace the role of Encourager, a decision that would expand my children's confidence exponentially.

Because my Type A personality runs deep, and the control freak in me still emerges from time to time, I have developed a foolproof way of putting control in its place. I pause and envision a moment in the future: I imagine my daughter in her first apartment, in a college classroom, or working at her first job when she encounters a problem. In the face of challenge and uncertainty, she is prepared, competent, and determined. Simply put, I am able to rein in my urge to micromanage by remembering the ultimate goal: to raise capable, independent adults who feel empathy for others, appreciate the blessings they have, and are empowered to keep reaching for what they want. Unfortunately, in the last decade, it seems many of us have lost sight of our primary responsibility: to raise kids who are prepared to tackle the world on their own with enough experience and confidence to do so. This shift from *actively* involved to *overly* involved has created debilitating issues for our kids.

In a recent study, Chris Segrin and Michelle Givertz sought to examine the association between parental overinvolvement and control and young adult identity, namely self-efficacy and psychological entitlement. Givertz makes a convincing argument for why parents need to be mindful that they are not doing beyond what is needed developmentally for their kids. "On the one hand, I think these are all well-intentioned parents who are invested in their children's lives. But it is stunting the growth of these young people and creating other problems for them, in terms of depression, anxiety and negative coping behaviors."[1]

Julie Lythcott-Haims, a former dean of freshmen and undergraduate advising at Stanford University, was so alarmed by the trend she was seeing in students that she wrote a book called, *How to Raise an Adult: Break Free of the Overparenting Trap and Prepare Your Kid for Success.* Of the students, Lythcott-Haims writes, "They were accomplished academically and had done a flurry of impressive activities, but they seemed to be reliant upon a parent to tell them what to do, how to do it, how to feel about it."[2] The students were far from the happy, capable young adults their parents had hoped to raise.

As more and more studies reveal the damaging trend of excessive parental involvement in the day-to-day lives of adolescents, nothing speaks quite as powerfully as the desires expressed by young people themselves. One of the top stressors kids report through my classroom Index Card Exercise is "lack of control" over their own lives. Many say they feel stifled by parents looking over their shoulder as they try to honor commitments, complete tasks, make mistakes, and take responsibility for their actions. During my classroom visits, young people often express the desire to develop their own opinions and to have their beliefs be heard, even if they differ from their parents' views. Read for yourself the many ways kids are expressing their desire to take command of their lives:

- *Parents seem to forget that we are capable of making good decisions.*
- *I wish my parents weren't always so worried. I just want to live life and be freer, but my parents are always so worried about me.*

1. Chris Segrin and Michelle Givertz, qtd. in La Monica Everett-Haynes, "The Dangers of 'Overparenting,'" *Medicalxpress*, March 20, 2013, https://medicalxpress.com /news/2013–03-dangers-overparenting.html.

2. Julie Lythcott-Hains, qtd. in Katrina Onstad, "Are We the Worst Generation of Parents Ever?" *Today's Parent*, January 8, 2016, https://www.todaysparent.com/family /are-we-the-worst-generation-of-parents/.

- *We need parents who accept the fact that we are learning; we aren't going to get everything right the first time.*
- *When kids ask to be alone, you need to give them space and time.*
- *From my parents I want support and requested guidance.*
- *Parenting your child isn't always about being mean and enforcing—sometimes you have to listen to what your kids feel is best over what you think is right.*
- *A lot of people underestimate what kids and teens can do, but also many kids and teens underestimate themselves.*
- *Parents, encourage your kids to follow their passions; our world will be better for it.*
- *I wish my parents knew that I can stand up for myself.*
- *When it comes to helping out our communities, kids can do everything adults can do—but we are not always given the chance.*
- *Parents need to understand that sometimes taking risks is okay and not everyone wants a solid future of some office job.*
- *Kids want more freedom and forgiveness from their parents.*
- *Just because we mess up doesn't mean we haven't learned from those mistakes.*
- *We are changing and growing, and parents need to let it happen because we cannot be your little babies forever.*

While it's safe to say most, if not all, parents want their children to thrive as adults, the pace and pressure of modern life are causing some parents to lose sight of this goal. Many parents allow their fear of the worst-case scenario to drive their parenting decisions, which, ironically, is what might drive their teens to some of these scenarios anyway. In some cases, kids are monitored and scheduled every minute of their lives, leaving little opportunity to make choices and take initiative toward their own interests or goals. Due to the hectic schedules of many families, Mom and Dad are less compelled to hold children to all of their household and academic responsibilities, and in some cases, pick up the slack for them. Caught up in our highly competitive, comparison-happy culture, these parents feel compelled to swoop in and rescue rather than allow natural consequences to play out. Some adults find the digital and academic world of adolescence so overwhelming and intimidating that they throw up their hands and allow their kids to do whatever they want. Some parents do *for* their kids because it's easier to avoid conflict and pushback. Fear for their kids' safety causes some parents to hover and protect to the point that they smother.

No matter the reasons, parents are failing to nurture their children's independence. One thing is clear: underestimating and undermining our children's capabilities hurts us all. It's essential for parents to challenge this new status quo and find a good balance between protecting and empowering while maintaining a connected relationship with their teen.

Now more than ever, we must accept the fact that independence is not something we can expect our children to know how to take for themselves; we must grant it. Providing an umbrella for teens to hide under might feel like the right move, but we have to know when to provide shelter and when to let them experience a little rain in hopes that it will better prepare them for larger storms. We can do that in several ways:

- By showing confidence in our kids' capabilities
- By releasing our kids to make decisions and experience the consequences (good and bad)
- By recognizing the wise choices our kids make and pointing out their strengths as they attempt tasks on their own
- By serving as a sounding board (rather than a fixer) as they weigh the pros and cons of certain decisions
- By modeling accountability and responsibility when we make poor decisions
- By allowing our kids to discover their own identity through trial and error

In the pages ahead, we'll explore strategies for nurturing seeds of independence through *Confidence, Communication,* and *Opportunity.*

When we support our kids in developing skills for independence, we are not only preparing them for life, but we are also instilling in them a vital sense of the value they bring to the world—value that comes from knowing they are making meaningful contributions only they can make. As satisfying as accolades, awards, and trophies can be, the rewards our kids earn when they contribute their inherent, unique gifts will add unshakable meaning to their lives and become true and lasting measures of success.

By committing to learn how to become an Encourager—rather than a manager, rescuer, permissive pleaser, or critic—we empower young people to live happy, productive lives. Belief, communication, and vision can be the gifts we give our kids, anchors they can rely on for strength when they question whether they have what it takes.

INDEPENDENCE THROUGH CONFIDENCE

My life skills lists were my claim to fame when I was a special education teacher of high school and elementary students. As soon as a student qualified for my services, their regular education teachers would pull me aside and ask how quickly the student could get one of *those lists*—their tones just a little suggestive, as though the lists were either illegal or held supernatural powers. Within the small Indiana school district where I worked, I developed a reputation for turning the most problematic students into capable ones. But it was not me; it was them. The students did all the work; they just needed a little confidence and direction to help them get there.

Although the unmet goals differed from student to student, the reason they failed to do what was expected of them fell into one of three categories: (1) they didn't know how to reach the goals; (2) they lacked the tools and confidence; or (3) the goals—such as "follow directions" and "get packed up"—were too vague.

My approach for equipping my students to succeed was twofold: I learned about their interests and passions, and then I pinpointed their strengths and motivations. Though the goal of most conversations was to discuss their areas of challenge and understand why they had difficulty meeting expectations, I was able to help them see how they could use their unique strengths to turn things around. Because I had done the work to learn what those unique strengths were before attempting to problem solve, I was able to use those traits to inspire, motivate, and empower them.

Focusing on a few problem areas at a time, the students and I would break down their goals into smaller steps and identify ways to practice new behaviors. If a tool or strategy was needed to curb a negative behavior or complete a routine task, I would also provide that. A critical piece of the process was that we made the lists together, so each list was customized to that particular student and rooted in a foundation of his or her strengths and interests. If he loved music, we would create a lyrical mantra to repeat when he needed it. If she loved drawing, she would sketch pictures of positive outcomes next to the written goals. If he loved superheroes, we would talk about the student's own "superpowers." The students' input was critical to success. It was their list, not mine. I was merely there to support and encourage them, which proved to be an important piece. My students actually looked forward to my classroom visits, when we'd review the progress on their self-monitored lists. Where there was success, we celebrated. Where there wasn't, we made a game plan. In both cases, we were a team.

Time after time, the parents of my students were shocked to see their kids getting in trouble less and accomplishing more. Perhaps it was the awareness of the problem, the clarity of the goal, or the positive expectation that made the difference. Perhaps it was the fact that they knew I'd be checking in, investing my time and attention in their success. Regardless of what initially created the student's motivation to change, something within them sustained it. *Feeling capable is powerful; knowing you achieved something with your own two hands is confidence-building.*

About twelve years after I'd stopped working with one of my most troubled students, he contacted me via social media.

"Remember, before you moved to Florida, how you told me I could make my own lists?" he asked. "Well, that is what I did." My former student proceeded to tell me he had recently been commended for his work with a national youth-led organization devoted to improving mental health services and resources for young people. This young man, whom many expected would spend time behind bars, had become a leader in his community and a positive role model for young people. After thanking me for believing in him, he once again mentioned the power of the lists. The hair on my arms stood up when he called them "road maps," which had taken him somewhere better than he'd ever expected to go.

My student's words provided the lifeline I needed to stay true to my commitment of being an empowering Encourager to my children rather than a controlling manager. I'd come to realize how triggering it was for me to have to repeat morning directions over and over. With every verbal reminder of an uncompleted task, frustration grew, tension rose, and dependency increased.

With my student's words fresh in my mind, I was inspired to do something different. One morning, rather than repeat myself for the fourth time, I grabbed a sticky note from the pencil drawer. I drew a picture of a lunchbox, a pair of shoes, a pair of glasses, and a water bottle, and handed it to then-five-year-old Avery. I'd drawn an empty checkbox next to each item.

"Here is your list. Check them off as you go. It is up to you if you miss the bus and we have to walk to school," I said matter-of-factly. I set the kitchen timer on the counter so she could see how much time she had.

I watched in awe as Avery went right to work. In less than two minutes, she stood by the door all packed up and ready to go. "Look! I even had time left!" she said, smiling. And that was the moment I knew life skills lists were about to become an integral part of our family's daily routine.

After brainstorming all the tasks they needed to accomplish each day, my daughters found it helpful to break down duties into morning and evening lists. Evening lists consisted of things such as doing homework, setting the dinner table, practicing instruments, making lunch, and selecting outfits for the next day. Morning lists consisted of things such as getting dressed; putting their snacks, lunches, and water bottles into their backpacks; brushing their hair; and putting on shoes.

Weekend lists included household chores, which I later called "contributions," thanks to Amy McCready, author of *The Me, Me, Me Epidemic*. Tasks included things such as folding laundry and putting it away, cleaning bedrooms and the basement toy area, and changing out the cat's litter box. At any time, a spontaneous sticky-note list could be handed to a child when something outside the usual routine needed to be accomplished. The beauty of the list is that I did not have to nag or remind. If it was on the list, it needed to be completed. My kids knew they could do the tasks when they wanted, but they could not do the things they wanted to do, including any activities with a screen or being with friends, until their contributions were made. Miraculously, things got done.

When I started being invited to speak at out-of-town conferences, I was most grateful for the lists. I did not worry about how things were going to run or who was going to cover day-to-day tasks. My kids had their lists, and *they* were the ones who kept things running smoothly. When Scott was also traveling for work, my mom would come stay at our house. I'll never forget her comment about how wonderful it was to support and encourage her granddaughters in their efforts rather than doing things for them. It reminded me so much of my role as a supportive educator.

As my kids have grown and matured, their lists have also evolved. In many cases, visual reminders are no longer needed; daily tasks are now habits, and consequences for not following through are simply understood. The foundation provided by the lists over the years is evident almost daily. Just like my former student, my kids have begun making their own lists. It is not uncommon to see informal lists on doors, bathroom mirrors, and tucked into binders. What brings me the most joy is seeing how my daughters' lists have become roadmaps, taking them to places far beyond our expectations.

Implemented with consistency, follow-through, guidance, and support, the Kid To-Do list can become an "I Can-Do" list they can carry along as they explore new paths paved with courage and confidence, paths that just might lead them to create:

Poetry
Song lyrics
Original recipes
Written prayers
Anchor quotes
Packing lists
Get well cards
Babysitting advertisements
Summer camp fliers
Vision boards

Lists aren't magic, but they are a magical tool for communicating a beautiful blend of guidance, expectation, belief, accountability, and encouragement, which brings me to this undeniable conclusion:

If you give a kid a list,
He knows what he needs to do.

If you give a kid a list,
She sees a pathway to a goal.

If you give a kid a list,
He hears: "I believe you can."

If you give a kid a list,
She just might start making her own.

If you give a kid a list,
Nagging turns to celebration.
Everyday tasks lead to extraordinary feats.

If you give a kid a list, you're offering belief.
And a kid can do great things with a little belief.

Decide this is the end of coddling, doubting, nagging, and repeating.
Instead, give a kid a list.
The path to independence has never been so clear.

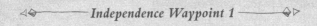 *Independence Waypoint 1*

A BETTER WAY

When it became clear that Avery's approach to life was gentler and more intentional than the rest of the world typically operates, I was faced with a dilemma. How could I embrace my child for who she is while also preparing her to manage expectations, deadlines, and responsibilities as a contributing member of society?

Again, for direction and perspective, I turned to my teacher training and experience. After some thought, here is what I realized I already knew:

- Giving my students tools to help them be successful was not an attack on their self-esteem; what *was* a blow to their confidence was *not* being able to manage or keep up.
- Providing my students with expectations and boundaries did not hinder or restrict them; expectations and boundaries provided a safe and consistent arena for them to thrive in.
- Addressing my students' troubled areas did not shatter their egos; it relieved them to know they had support in overcoming their struggles.

I knew that every one of my students had a desire to be capable in everyday life—they just didn't always have the tools, support, or motivation to get there. Thinking about this helped me investigate how I could best help my Noticer child in ways that would equip her for life while also preserving her unique way of being in the world.

I discovered that Avery responded best to expectations if she was able to give input. "What do you think we should do about this problem?" was a question that brought forth novel ideas for success. Leaving this question for her to solve motivated her to create tools to help her complete expected tasks—tools that were drawn from and therefore resonated with her musical and artistic nature. She started using rhymes, color-coded notes, sand timers, and weekly calendars so she knew what was coming up. Her goal was to complete afternoon and evening duties on her list by 8:15 p.m. because she enjoyed having downtime each evening. This allowed us time to watch a show together, play a game, or for her to use her electronic device.

Avery was also the one who decided it would be helpful to note exactly how long it took her to complete each morning task. Once she realized she was taking twenty minutes to get dressed, which left only three minutes to eat (definitely not her style), she was motivated to get dressed in half the time. This shift not only helped the whole morning run more smoothly, but it clearly helped her learn something *on her own* about time management.

Time was the commodity that allowed Avery to both *be herself* and *realize her capability*, so factoring in extra time, doing things the night before, and having unscheduled time was a welcome and now integral part of the daily plan.

Watching Avery use the tools she developed to be responsible gave me the opportunity to consistently point out her strengths, but that was not all. Being exposed to the way my child, the Noticer, approached things helped me learn the value of taking time to put thought, care, and love into daily tasks.

The first time I internalized this was when I'd retrieved Avery's flowered suitcase from the basement for a trip to see family in Indiana. Knowing she needed to pack a week's worth of clothes, I was hesitant to give her the task. But instead of telling myself it would just be faster and easier if I did it, I decided it was time to let my then ten-year-old pack her own things.

After providing Avery with a general list of the items she needed to pack, I left the room. I'll admit, my expectations were not high, so when I saw her sitting on the couch ninety minutes later, I assumed she'd left the job incomplete, expecting that her highly efficient mother would finish up for her. But when I walked into Avery's room, my jaw dropped. I saw matching outfits laid out, blank lines filled in on the packing list, and sun hats and sunglasses (which weren't even on the list).

"See how I rolled my T-shirts?" Avery asked proudly as she joined me. "I saw that on a travel show. It saves room. You should try it."

"You never cease to show me a better way," I said, becoming emotional. I thought of the way Avery cuts fresh vegetables into easy-to-eat strips and packs them into reusable zipper snack bags to save the environment. I thought of the way she stops to sprinkle cinnamon on her applesauce because, "That's what Meme always does." I thought of the way she always waits for her grandpa, a polio survivor, so he doesn't walk alone.

Fast and efficient isn't always best, I thought as I thanked God for this child who, by staying true to who she is, shows others a better way.

As Avery proudly zipped up her neatly packed suitcase, I got a glimpse of the future. This creative musician with a big heart for animals and elderly people would travel the world with a guitar strapped on her back. In her hand, she would carry the bag she had confidently packed. The sights of her adventures would be extra beautiful, the new foods she tasted would taste even sweeter, and the experiences she had would be more fulfilling.

Why?

Because our most rewarding destinations are the ones we reach with our own two feet, in our own unique way.

Even as adults, we often don't know how to do what needs done in order to get where we're going. Those are the moments when we should allow ourselves to feel comfortable admitting we don't have all of the answers and lean humbly on each other to ask, *What do you think? How would you do it?*

It's a beautiful approach that will take you places you never thought you'd go.

INDEPENDENCE THROUGH COMMUNICATION

I felt honored when Dr. Shefali Tsabary, one of the world's most respected parenting educators, asked me to review her *#endshame* video a few years ago, a video she hoped would raise awareness about the trending practice of parents shaming their children on social media. I expected to be enlightened by Dr. Shefali's insights, but what occurred was nothing short of an emotional breakthrough.

Two minutes and twenty seconds into the video, Dr. Shefali spoke these words from a child's point of view: "I came to you so you could honor my soul, nurture my worth, and preserve my spirit. Yet it is you who annihilates my very essence in the name of parenting, in the name of love, in the name of teaching."

Still speaking from the child's perspective, Dr. Shefali then calls on parents to "become the person you were meant to be: the parent, the guardian, the usherer of my soul."

Although I was not one to shame my children publicly, I was quite the expert behind closed doors—particularly when it came to mistakes. Any time one of my children made an innocent mistake, I met that mistake with impatience, exasperation, and even eye rolls. I responded with the message, *You should know better.* But they were children. They were learning, and I seemed to forget that.

Although I'd made significant progress at accepting my kids *for who they were* so they could develop into their most authentic selves, Dr. Shefali's video had such a strong impact on me that I knew I had more work to do. Given that our family had just made its sixth move in a span of fourteen years, I decided it was time to do something I'd been longing to do forever: let go of the unnecessary expectations I put on myself to do it all and be it all. This move was my chance to start over with breathing room, healthy boundaries, and loving self-care practices I had never made time for in the past.

The practice of consistently saying yes to my heart's longings for several consecutive months released a long-held internal pressure. I felt lighter, happier, and more at peace than I had in my former community where our family had lived for six years. One night, I spontaneously asked Natalie if our new place was starting to feel like home. Natalie said something I'll never forget:

"I can breathe here."

Yes, this was a less competitive community. Yes, unique differences were more widely accepted. Yes, our family did not know many people, and therefore, we had fewer social obligations—but I couldn't help but believe it was the change in me that had the most influence on my child's ability to breathe. In my efforts to put less pressure on myself, I was also learning how to put less pressure on my daughter. I'd stopped commenting on Natalie's appearance and physique. I listened to her casual banter with no judgment, just presence. I waited until she asked for my help or my opinion. I stopped being quick to dissuade or disagree when Natalie talked about ambitious future plans or differing opinions.

I paid close attention to the way I responded to Natalie's adventurous way of doing things and the mistakes she made while trying. Excited by my determination to lay the groundwork to be a trusted confidant for bigger issues in her life, I also began reflecting back on our conversations. I wanted to gauge if I was leaving my daughter feeling encouraged after spending time with me. I noticed what assurances brought relief to her face and said them more. All these small changes led to greater connection. As my daughter opened up to me more and more, I recognized my own deep desire to be the one my child turns to in times of trouble. I knew that as she grew, the mistakes would come with greater costs and harder falls; I never wanted her to feel that she was alone in her most desolate hour.

Little did I know, that time would come sooner than expected.

One evening, as Natalie was getting ready for bed, words came from my child's mouth that I never thought I'd hear. I felt like I could not breathe. I had been sucker-punched. I was greatly disappointed by her choice, but there was a silver lining, and it was a major one: she was telling me.

This infraction was something she could easily have kept to herself and carried as a burden on her soul for many years. But just as I'd listened without judgment to her running commentary the day before, when she'd gone on about our cat's antics, I vowed to stay calm so our line of communication could remain open for hard conversations in the future.

Before I responded, I told myself:

Do not overreact.

Do not cry.

Do not threaten.

Do not belittle.

Do not act like you've never made a mistake.

In that moment, a shameful incident from my past came back to me. I thought, *What would I have wanted someone to say to me?*

"I am glad you told me this," I whispered to my distraught child. "Keeping it inside is harmful. You did the right thing by talking to me. I want you to know that other young people have made this same poor choice."

My daughter's hanging head abruptly lifted. "They have?"

I saw pent-up air expel from her chest as a weight was lifted. She was not the only one. She was not alone.

This was a pivotal moment. Although I would have had every right to punish her, to take away her freedoms, to lecture her on rights and wrongs, I didn't. I thought of that shameful moment from my teen years again.

I'd just started driving myself to school when I got pulled over for speeding. As if getting stopped by the police on a busy thoroughfare wasn't humiliating enough, I saw my dad drive past the scene on his way to work. The whole day, I felt sick thinking about what was going to happen when I got home. Later that night, Dad said he saw me pulled over. He did not guilt, berate, or belittle me. He talked to me about the repercussions of speeding and what the consequences would be if I was caught speeding again. Although I got his message loud and clear, there was understanding in his eyes. My dad could see I was beating myself up enough, and it was not necessary to add to my pain.

This solitary response changed the way I saw my dad from that moment on; I saw him as an ally to turn to in times of trouble, not a holier-than-thou authoritarian to fear and hide from. And that is exactly who I chose to be for Natalie in her moment of shame.

Yes, I told my daughter of my disappointment. Yes, I let her know she'd have to earn back my trust. Yes, I outlined some changes to prevent future issues, but I did not shame or forsake my daughter in her time of need. I did not kick her while she was down. I opened my arms, and we held each other.

This gesture answered a burning question I'd carried since the day I'd harshly blamed Natalie for her sister's fall on the library book. That was the day when Natalie's eyes held the unmistakable look of defeat—that no matter what she said, I would assume the worst about her. From that moment on, I'd wondered if I could become the type of parent a child could confide in. I wondered if I would be able to say the most loving words when I was most disappointed. I wondered if I would be able to stand with my child even when I felt betrayed. I wondered if I'd be able to hold my child when my broken heart wanted to push her away.

By the grace of God, I discovered that the answer to those questions was yes. Yes. I would.

"Listen," I said firmly. "No matter what mistakes you make today, tomorrow, or throughout your life, I will always love you. I will never turn my back on you. We can get through anything together. Okay?"

In the moment when I could have crushed my child's spirit, I supported her.

In the moment when I could have made her doubt herself, I reminded her she was human.

In the moment when I could have taught her a harsh lesson, I taught her a lesson of grace, a lesson of trust, a lesson of unconditional, everlasting love.

I know I won't always choose a loving response in the face of struggle as my daughter grows, but I will give my best effort. I will remind myself that all kids find themselves in difficult situations at some point. Situations that could probably be resolved or worked through with guidance and support from a trusted adult. However, if kids have been shut down when they faltered in the past, they will be far less likely to ask for help. They need to feel comfortable enough to come to us with all of it—the good, the bad, the confusing, the embarrassing, and the scary. Therefore, let's make it a daily practice to communicate in ways that open up, build trust, and restore connection.

May we always keep these truths in the forefront of our hopeful hearts:

We have the power to teach our kids a lesson.
We have the power to make them regret a poor choice.
We have the power to ensure they never forget what
    they've done.

We do.
But we also have the power to open a door for difficult future conversations.

We have the power to be a calm and supportive presence in their time of need.

We have the power to prevent a shameful experience from leaving a scar.

We have the power to prevent them from doing something permanent to stop the pain.

Let us not kick our kids when they are down.

Instead . . .

Let's reach out our hands and help them up.

Let's hug them tight and say, "I will not take my love away."

Let's respond to their mistakes the way we'd want someone to respond to ours.

In doing so, we might just become the person they need most . . .

The guardian of her heart.

The usherer of his soul.

The safe haven in a world too quick to destroy what is most precious in the click of a button.

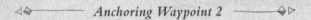

Anchoring Waypoint 2

THE KEY TO RECONNECTING

The phrase "Only love today" was a life-changing mantra that came to me during prayer and helped me make a permanent shift from a critical inner dialogue to a more loving, compassionate one. Whenever a critical thought came to my mind or my mouth, I cut it off with "Only love today." Sometimes I said it a thousand times a day, but it worked. Through it, I grasped a powerful truth that may have saved my relationship with my firstborn daughter: *Just because a critical thought comes to mind doesn't mean I have to speak it, act on it, or pass it on to someone I love. I can acknowledge that negative thought, and then let it go so something hopeful, helpful, or healing can take its place.*

With this realization, I was able to step back and let Natalie do for herself without judgment, commentary, or critique. As I began incorporating these pauses, I noticed Natalie often pinpointed and fixed the problems herself. As she was learning and growing, she thrived on having room to try, stumble, and try again without someone monitoring her.

To help expand my ability to repair the damage of Natalie's early years, I studied the rules for validation as taught by author and parenting coach Sandy Blackard: "No fixing, no judging (good or bad), no teaching, no questions. This is the step of connection. When you leave out fixing, judging, teaching, and questions, all that's left is pure understanding and compassionate listening. It's the key to reconnecting."[3]

Keeping those rules for validation in mind when I felt the need to dictate, criticize, or manage my children, spouse, or myself created moments of connection rather than moments of destruction. I've watched Natalie become more self-assured, more independent, and more joyful as I have practiced these rules.

Thanks to Sandy, I've learned there is great power in not sharing all the suggestions that instinctively pop into my mind, unless I know my suggestions will feel like help to my loved ones. "By listening and letting children solve their own problems, they learn how to get along without your intervention, which you can then point out as a strength," Sandy writes in *Say What You See for Teachers and Parents*.[4]

Although I made every effort to allow Natalie to identify her own problems and to pick my battles, there were times when I had to provide feedback about damaging patterns that needed to be addressed. One such issue arose as she was adjusting

3. Sandy Blackard, "How to Help a Perfectionist Child," *Language of Listening* (blog), https://www.languageoflistening.com/how-to-help-a-perfectionist-child/.

4. Sandy Blackard, "If Kids Fighting Makes You Mad," *Language of Listening* (blog), https://www.languageoflistening.com/if-kids-fighting-makes-you-mad.

to the rigors of a high school curriculum while swimming on the school swim team. Although I had my own ideas about how to remedy this situation, backed by compelling research on the importance of sleep for teens, I used Sandy's approach when raising my concerns with my daughter.

"I've noticed you've been staying up quite late getting your work finished, and I worry about you. How are you feeling about things?" I asked gently.

What began as a slightly defensive response turned into a lengthy talk, a verbal exhale of the pressure and the concerns she was feeling. I learned things I did not know about her classes, how well she was planning, and how hard she was working.

Sandy's approach enabled me to learn these things I did not know—and would not have found out if I had acted like the one with the answers.

From my tone, my words, and my willingness to listen, Natalie could see I was an ally, that we were on the same team, rooting for her to live a healthy life while doing the things she needed to do.

I asked questions:

"How can I help?"

"What might be some ways to get to bed even thirty minutes earlier?"

Each question brought further enlightenment and offered her the chance to see that my intention was to offer support, not criticism.

So often, I am reminded that I am learning along with my daughter, and that feels really good, considering the way I started out. It still pains me to think of the ideas, discussions, and opportunities to thrive that I shut down by my earlier efforts.

But I choose to live in today. And I am learning there are

helpful, healing ways to have difficult discussions with the people I love.

Rather than jumping in with what we *think* we know, we can try:

Asking a question

Listening

Supporting

Honoring

Respecting

Encouraging through our words and body language.

We might find that a heavy issue is not so heavy when we choose to carry it *with* our kids, rather than *for* them.

INDEPENDENCE THROUGH OPPORTUNITY

I imagined my daughters being asked, "What fun things did you do over the summer?" when they began a new school year after The Summer of Mom's Giant Kidney Stone.

Their responses would be less than stellar, paling in comparison to their peers' exciting adventures. Because sometimes summer is not about having fun; sometimes summer is about survival.

I knew this in my heart, yet at the same time, I couldn't seem to get past Guilt's critical voice in my head:

You should be playing more.

You should be planning more.

You should be having more fun.

Your kids aren't going to be under your roof forever, you know.

For far too many years, I'd accepted Guilt's critical words as truths, letting them derail me from embracing the precious moments at hand. So, when I realized Guilt was getting the best of me, I knew I needed to diminish its power by talking to someone I knew would understand.

I turned to my mom and, holding nothing back, lamented how incredibly guilty I felt that Natalie and Avery's summer had been so dismal.

"Don't you remember?" Mom asked emphatically. "Don't you remember how I worked all day while you and your sister took care of yourselves during the summer months?"

Yes, I remembered. I thought it was cool that my sister, Rebecca, and I were in charge of ourselves. I thought it was *not cool* that we were expected to complete daily duties that improved our home, minds, bodies, and personal savings accounts. Although I did not like these job responsibilities, I fulfilled them faithfully.

Rebecca and I would spend the morning getting our tasks completed so we could ride our bikes to the neighborhood pool in the afternoon. We'd put sunscreen on each other's backs before we left the house and carry our towels and goggles in a drawstring bag. There was no one there to remind us to collect our belongings when we left the pool—we just did it. And if we forgot something, we hoped it would end up in the Lost and Found—otherwise, we'd spend our hard-earned money to replace the missing item.

One of my evening duties was cutting the vegetables for the dinner salad around the time my mom would come home from work. I would listen to my parents talk about the families my mom worked with—families in crisis. It was her job to provide mental health services and support to vulnerable adults who wanted to keep their families intact. It was my job to make the salad, but I knew I wanted a job like Mom's someday—one that made a difference.

I remember feeling my mom's presence whenever I stepped into the kitchen pantry to make myself breakfast and lunch. Mom bought things I liked and foods that were healthy for me. I felt my mom's presence in the little smiley face notes that she left for Rebecca and me in random places, celebrating jobs well done.

I remember Mom being gone, but she was never absent. I felt her presence even when she was at work. And when my mom was around, she did something that made me take pause. She said, "I love you," a lot, right out of the blue.

While riding in the car, she'd call out, "I love you." I'd see my mom's big, brown eyes smiling at me through her oversized glasses in the rearview mirror.

In the morning, when I groggily poured milk on my cereal, she'd say "I love you," as if my bedhead was a beautiful sight to behold.

Because our time together was limited, I think my mom said the words "I love you" when she *felt* them rather than when it was expected. Most people I knew reserved that three-word phrase for special occasions, departures, achievements, or bedtime—but not my mom. Her affirmations of love for us were spontaneous. She just put it out there. And because the phrase was never surrounded by any other words and never tied to conditions or expectations, it was accentuated, heard, and absorbed.

That's probably what I remember most about my mom, who was gone a lot but not absent. I remember the unprompted "I love you" that hung in the air, mine for the taking as I set off on my path of independence.

"Yes, I remember the summers when you had to work all day," I told my seventy-four-year-old mom after admitting that guilt was getting the best of me.

"Sometimes I left before you were awake and didn't get home until dinnertime or later," Mom elaborated. "You and Rebecca learned to manage your time, make meals, and keep up a house. And you two turned out just fine, in my opinion," she added, as if ready to take on anyone who might disagree.

Shortly after my mom and I had this conversation, I came across an article on overparenting and how it correlates with the current mental health crisis on college campuses. The results of the studies described in the article quickly put guilt in its place and reinforced my mom's view. Children who perform daily life skills tasks and have the opportunity to make decisions for themselves are more likely to become capable and self-reliant adults. I was particularly struck by this section of the article:

> When parents have tended to do the stuff of life for kids— the waking up, the transporting, the reminding about deadlines and obligations, the bill-paying, the question-asking, the decision-making, the responsibility-taking, the talking to strangers, and the confronting of authorities, kids may be in for quite a shock when parents turn them loose in the world of college or work. They will experience setbacks, which will feel to them like failure. Lurking beneath the problem of whatever thing needs to be handled is the student's inability to differentiate the self from the parent.[5]

After reading the article several times, I reflected back on the events of the summer with a fresh perspective. Between keeping up with medical appointments, recovering from two surgeries, and preparing for a book release, our summer had been a far cry from the fun-loving one I'd hoped my kids would have. Guilt wanted me to think about everything my children had missed because of the health challenge I'd been through. But after that clarifying and encouraging conversation with my mom, I hung up the phone and, through teary eyes, I saw something guilt didn't want me to see—things that probably wouldn't have happened without the freedom and the opportunity for my kids to *do for themselves*.

I saw kids who held two full weeks of camps for neighborhood

---

5. Julie Lythcott-Haims, "Kids of Helicopter Parents Are Sputtering Out," *Slate* (website), July 5, 2015, https://slate.com/human-interest/2015/07/helicopter-parenting -is-increasingly-correlated-with-college-age-depression-and-anxiety.html.

kids in and out of the basement of our home. I saw kids who planned and managed a mini market with friends on a Saturday morning. I saw kids who got quite good at making beds . . . kids who attempted and failed at French macarons but had fun trying . . . kids who finally caught on to hanging up wet towels after several unsuccessful years . . . kids who became expert laundry folders . . . kids who could order and pay for their food without adult assistance . . . kids who fixed a delicious hot lunch and cleaned up afterward . . . kids who could entertain themselves for hours with a little dish soap and a Slip 'N Slide . . . kids who came to my bedside each night to have Talk Time because I was not physically able to come to theirs.

When I look back on that summer now, I see something that looks an awful lot like the gifts my sister and I were given: the gift of independence . . . the gift of learning from our mistakes . . . the gift of confidence . . . the gift of collaboration that reinforced an emotional connection between us . . . the gift of doing something with our own two hands.

The Summer of Mom's Giant Kidney Stone wasn't an activity-packed summer; there was no celebration for crossing off all the items on our summer bucket list; in truth, there wasn't even a list that summer, but that didn't mean that summer was squandered time. There were lots of gifts—lessons that likely won't be apparent until my grown children are standing in their first apartment or place of employment and know exactly what to do without any help from me.

I think it's high time I stop calling it The Summer of Mom's Giant Kidney Stone and instead refer to it as The Summer of I Loved You.

I loved you so much I let you do for yourself.

I loved you so much I let you make a mess and clean it up.

I loved you so much I let you fail and try again without my commentary.

I loved you so much I did not manage your time, but let you manage your own.

I loved you so much I let you make decisions and hold yourself accountable, no matter the result.

Where there's less nagging, reminding, and instructing, there's more love. May our kids grab hold of these opportunities to grow with capable and eager hands, holding our love closely to their chests as they progress on their path toward independence.

◁❧ ——— *Anchoring Waypoint 3* ——— ❧▷

THIS COULD GET UNCOMFORTABLE

The work required to teach our kids independence is hard, and although the end result often creates a sense of pride in both the adult and the young person, it is normal to expect many uncomfortable emotions along the way. Feelings like anxiety, fear, annoyance, guilt, rejection, and uncertainty are all emotions we may experience as we practice allowing our kids to learn, discover, and navigate the world on their own. When experiencing these feelings of unease, I find it helpful and healing to try to figure out the cause of my internal conflict. This practice, along with accepting these feelings as neither bad nor good, helps me move toward overcoming one of the most painful necessities of parenting—letting go.

As my daughters have entered the preteen and teen years, I am now faced with opportunities to practice this necessity on a near-daily basis. One recent Sunday, I was out for a walk when Natalie sent me a text. She wanted to make yeast rolls for Scott's birthday dinner, and the yeast in the cabinet was old.

"Could you take me to the store when you get home?" she asked.

I grumbled to myself. I sensed the whole excursion would be a waste of time and money. Making yeast rolls is a delicate and complicated process, even for the most experienced baker. I quickly decided there was no way Natalie could pull that off. Not to mention, I'd just finished cleaning the whole kitchen!

I decided that when I got home, I'd tell her how hard it is. "Why not make muffins?" I would suggest.

When I arrived home forty-five minutes later, there she was, deep into dough. Flour, yeast, sugar, and baking utensils surrounded her.

"Dad took me to the store so I could get started," a flour-dusted Natalie said with a smile as she stirred the massive lump in the bowl with determination.

Quietly, I got to work on the cream cheese icing for Scott's birthday cake. Natalie was in a talkative mood and chatted me up about the bread machine I used to have.

"It did all this?" she said in awe, stretching her floury hands out wide.

"Yep," I said, suddenly appreciating that trusty old bread machine in a way I hadn't before.

"Now I have to knead," Natalie said as she generously sprinkled the counter with flour. I refrained from cringing as flour fell onto my sparkling clean floor.

For what seemed like an eternity, Natalie punched and flipped, punched and flipped, making the most noise a human can possibly make with a blob of dough.

I looked up at Scott, who was watching his favorite football team play on TV. If the noise bothered him, he sure didn't show it.

I kept quiet, but my brain said, *There's no way these rolls are going to be edible.*

"I can't wait to see how they turn out," Natalie said excitedly.

I watched as she took a pink highlighter and marked off another line in the recipe she'd printed out. Cleverly, she was highlighting each step as she went, so she wouldn't miss a step in the process.

"I tried to make yeast bread from scratch once," I confessed. "It turned out like a brick. Maybe if I had done something like what you are doing, it would have been better."

Natalie explained the rising process to me. She suspected that I rushed the process.

"*Who, me?*" I said.

We both chuckled. My daughter knows me well.

A few hours later, with absolutely no help from me, Natalie pulled from the oven the most beautiful yeast rolls I'd ever laid eyes on.

She handed me a piece to taste.

I took a bite, and my mouth began rejoicing. "Natalie!" I exclaimed. "These are as good as Meme's rolls—and you know my mom makes the best rolls ever!"

Natalie glowed with pride.

At dinner, the whole family marveled over Natalie's golden-brown masterpieces. Scott told Natalie to make sure and save the recipe.

As I took a photo of Natalie and her rolls to send to my mom, I felt a tinge of sadness for doubting her. I felt guilty for being so negative. But before I threw myself completely under the bus, I noted the progress: I'd kept my mouth shut—me, the woman who used to burst her kids' bubbles before they even tried. Me, the woman who control-freaked the joy out of their attempts to be independent. Me, the woman who deemed her kids' ambitions too far-fetched based solely on the inconvenience/mess factor.

Yes, there was progress—both in my response to my

children's efforts *and* in accepting and understanding my own uncomfortable feelings about these efforts.

Having doubts is not a crime; it's human nature. I have reservations and self-centered thoughts regarding my children's ambitions on a regular basis, but now I catch myself long enough to consider that what seems impossible for them might just be my past experience talking. Just because something didn't go well for me doesn't mean it won't go well for them. As hard as it is to keep my mouth shut, I always learn a thing or two if I do.

I am well aware that I have many years ahead wherein my kids will fight for their independence, and it will not only be inconvenient and messy but greatly worrisome and, at times, offensive and painful. In those moments, I will consider the alternative: a young adult who never wants to leave the house and the shelter of her parents' instruction. It will serve me well to remember that a young person exerting control over her own choices—even when it is not pleasant and feels like pushback—is a vital part of growing into adulthood.

And should all else fail, I will refer to what may be the most profound words ever written about an adult's place in a child's miraculous journey:

> Childhood isn't a time when he is molded into a human who will then live life; he is a human who is living life. No child will miss the zest and joy of living unless these are denied him by adults who have convinced themselves that childhood is a period of preparation.
>
> How much heartache we would save ourselves if we would recognize the child as a partner with adults in the process of living, rather than always viewing him as an apprentice. How much we would teach each other—adults

with the experience and children with the freshness. How full both our lives could be.[6]

John Taylor's words contain pressure-relieving wisdom for a nourishing life. We need not know it all or control it all—we receive far more of what we all need when we partner, listen, and learn. So let spontaneous ideas unfold. Let flour dust fall where it may. Let unlimited tries be given and mistakes be made. Let confidence rise and laughter ensue. Who knows? We might just get to taste the goodness of life that once seemed impossible to reach.

LIVE LOVE NOW REFLECTION: THE DIRECTION OF LOVE

As I pulled the car into dense, early morning traffic to head to the orthopedist's office, Avery's hand flew to her face.

"Oh no! Socks!" Meaning, she'd grabbed her shoes to put on in the car, but no socks.

I'm all for personal responsibility and natural consequences, but I also believe in grace, understanding, and helping someone out when they are already down. Simultaneously finding out you'll be wearing a scoliosis brace until you stop growing and will likely need surgery for the structural issues in your foot can bring a person pretty far down.

"You can have mine," I said without hesitation. "I'll take them off when we get there."

My daughter's sigh of relief did not escape my notice.

"Thanks, Mom," she said.

Avery didn't utter one word about the socks probably not matching or being way too big or maybe even being sweaty—she

---

6. John A. Taylor, *Notes on an Unhurried Journey* (New York: Four Walls Eight Windows, 1991), 310.

just expressed gratitude, because when you're walking into uncertain territory, you'll take whatever familiar comforts you can get, even if they're not ideal.

I'd planned to put on another pair of socks as soon as I got home from the appointment, but with a writing deadline hovering over me, I dove right into work. Around noon, I noticed how uncomfortable my sockless feet had become.

I looked down at my bare feet in those running shoes, and I felt something I don't often feel—validated.

I don't know if we, as human beings, fully realize how many comforts, assurances, and barely noticeable breaths of oxygen we offer to the people we love each day. I don't know if we fully realize how often we decide to choose love when we could choose one of many other alternatives. All day long, we must discern when to stand firm and when to be flexible, when to be direct and when to ask questions, when to speak up and when to be silent, when to be supportive and when to step back. Whenever we make the wrong choice, we berate ourselves. But what about when we make the right choices? We make those, too—we make right choices all day long; we just don't seem to stop and take notice.

Well, on that one unseasonably warm afternoon in April, I noticed. It was impossible not to, actually. And rather than being quick to fix my discomfort, I relished it for just a moment and allowed myself to celebrate the impact of my sock loan on my daughter's day, an opportunity that is quite rare during this exhausting, baffling, sometimes downright terrifying journey of raising humans.

I was sockless and uncertain, but I was not hopeless or without direction.

Why?

Because . . .

Love is an anchor that steadies.

Love is a road map that guides.

Love is a blanket that warms.

Love is a brace that supports.

Love is a balm that heals.

And sometimes, love is a pair of mismatched socks that relieves.

All day, I thought about my middle schooler navigating a long testing day at school after having to go to her sixth medical appointment in a month's time. I hoped and prayed she felt comforted whenever she looked down. Because there, on her aching feet, were her mama's socks, reminding her that she will never walk alone.

That's what love does.

REFLECTION QUESTIONS

1. Overall, how would you describe the balance between requiring obedience and allowing freedom in your parenting? Which do you tend to rely on more? In what areas, if any, would you like to approach things differently?

2. If you were to release yourself from the role of manager, what do you fear might result? What might you gain?

3. Over the past week, how often would you say you allowed your adolescent to feel the power of responsibility, make choices, and/or solve problems in order to discover his or her own identity? In what ways might you give your teen even more autonomy during the week ahead?

4. What do you want to see when you envision your adolescent as a young adult? How does this match what he or she envisions for him or herself? How might you move toward supporting your adolescent's aspirations while also helping him or her develop self-governing skills?

5. When recently did you choose love when you could have chosen something else? Take a moment and recognize the significance of it. What other "right" choices can you affirm?

PART 3

BE A GUIDE, NOT A HALF-LISTENER

Guides...

- Nurture conditions that allow others to learn lessons that will prepare them for the path ahead.
- Model how to cope with conflict, change, and adversity.
- Cultivate sound decision-making by gathering information to verify facts, weighing pros and cons, considering different perspectives, and analyzing the impact of possible outcomes.
- Teach critical thinking, which is thinking infused with curiosity and integrity.
- Show vulnerability by sharing past failures that produced valuable insights they were able to call upon in the future.
- Recognize failure as an opportunity to learn, grow, and, in some cases, redirect one's path without giving up.
- Understand the importance of listening to one's internal compass in order to honor one's truest self, deepest hopes, and greatest values.
- Ground themselves in honesty, authenticity, and reliability.
- Serve as a lighthouse, a safe haven, or a respite for those in need of relief from the world's judgments, pressures, threats, dangers, and demands.

CHAPTER 5

WORRIED

What light can you shed by sharing your dark places?
It is time to give your pain purpose. Time to put work
boots on it. Send it out into the world. Give it a job.

—Laura Parrott Perry, *Freedom Song*

One of the summer expectations my parents set for my sister and me when we were growing up was to take a two-mile walk every day. Because my parents were both at work, this practice was purely on the honor system.

"How was your walk today?" my mom would ask when she got home.

"Fine," I'd usually say, often thinking how easy it would be to not go and just say I had.

But I never did that.

Every single day, without fail, I walked the same two-mile loop around the neighborhood. It didn't matter if it was sweltering outside or if dark clouds threatened rain; I laced up my shoes and set out—not because I was an obedient child, but because walking made me feel better.

Walking was so therapeutic that I continued this daily practice throughout high school, college, wedding plans, teaching days, a miscarriage, two pregnancies, and published book after book after book. Year after year, I walked through angst, pain, worry, and doubt. Through breezes and birdsong, I heard God's guidance. Through the rhythmic sound of my feet upon the ground, I felt hope emerge. Through the sun's warmth, my soul strengthened as the treads of my shoes wore thin.

Hoping that walking might one day ease my daughters' anxieties too, I invited them to join me as they grew.

Most of the time, they declined the invitation, but my heart was adamant that I should not stop asking.

And then, one day, it happened. Not only did one of my daughters say yes, but from that point forward, she began inviting *me* to go with *her*.

"Will you walk with me tonight?" Natalie began asking quite regularly around age thirteen. Her requests usually came after 8 p.m., when I was bone tired and had just put my feet up. Nevertheless, I slipped on my shoes. The crisp night air acted as a stimulant for conversation, affording me a precious opportunity to hear what was weighing on my daughter's heart.

One particular walk Natalie and I shared during a holiday break is especially memorable. Our family had been joined by my parents and my sister on the South Carolina coast, where I'd celebrated countless Christmases growing up. I'd walked that same stretch of beach countless times by myself over a twenty-year period, but it felt a bit surreal to have my daughter walk the same path beside me.

During the first mile, Natalie and I discussed a wide array of topics—her thirst for travel, her plans for making money to put toward buying a car, what high school would be like, what she would be doing for New Year's Eve, and cats; we always discussed our cats.

As the conversation trailed off, Natalie said, "Tell me a story."

Looking out into the vast ocean, I was reminded of an experience

I'd had spotting a stranded alligator while walking the beaches of the Gulf Coast earlier that fall. The animal was quite small and couldn't seem to escape the waves that continually battered him. I couldn't tell if he was trying to come ashore or go out into the ocean, but it was clear he was stuck, all alone, in what I'm sure to him felt like an impossible predicament. Although I stood there not knowing how to help, I knew in my heart that I could not walk by.

Hoping that two heads were better than one, I decided to stop a passerby to see if she had any thoughts on the situation. The woman was also concerned but equally unsure what to do.

After watching the helpless gator get tossed back and forth in the whitewash of the waves for several minutes, the woman unexpectedly asked about the pocket-size notebook I was holding.

I told her I was an author whose best ideas come during walks. Feeling surprisingly comfortable with her, I shared more than usual. "The books I write are about being fully present in life, so you notice opportunities to love and be loved, even when it's difficult or inconvenient—kind of like noticing struggling baby alligators and trying to help them," I said, smiling.

"To notice and respond with love," the woman repeated.

Sensing she was open to more, I said, "I believe it's the opportunities for connection that we miss or walk by that create our largest points of pain, turmoil, and regret. It is when we find it in our nature to notice and respond with love that we bring peace, healing, and purpose to our lives."

That notion is what led me to respond to the alligator's plight.

After declaring she was going to look up my books as soon as she got home, the woman went on her way. I consulted a few more beach walkers to no avail. Finally, I took matters into my own hands and called the Department of Natural Resources. I spoke to a man named Mark who assured me the alligator could survive a few days in the ocean. He explained that reptiles go into the saltwater to rid themselves of parasites.

"Don't worry; he'll be okay," Mark said assuredly.

Snapping me back to the current moment, Natalie teased, "Mom, only you would try to save an alligator."

I felt a sudden twinge of joy knowing Natalie thought of me as an animal advocate and that there was no creature too obscure, too small, or too troubled for my support. My parents had made similar observations when I was a girl. It was not uncommon for me to carry housebound spiders safely outside, stop to assist turtles across the street, and spend hours placing washed-up starfish back in the ocean so they wouldn't perish.

"I lost that part of myself for a while," I admitted to Natalie, not feeling inclined to elaborate.

"I know," Natalie said quietly, with nothing but love in her voice. We walked back to the rental in silence but deeply connected by our conversation, both scanning the vast water, hoping to catch a glimpse of someone or something in need of loving attention.

Later that same night, in the condo, I showed my dad one of the videos from a new online course I was about to launch. I explained how each week, participants would receive a video of me sharing a painful truth from my life that became a catalyst for change. I told him how I believed in this approach because in order to face the fears preventing us from truly living and loving, we have to first tap into some very hard truths about ourselves. I explained that in response to each truth, rather than excusing or pushing the pain and discomfort away, I allowed it to lead and enlighten me. And I told him how this process had changed my life.

In the video I shared with my dad, I was describing a painful truth triggered by the look of fear I saw in Natalie's eyes at age seven after she spilled a bag of rice all over the floor. Upon hearing her name mentioned in the video, Natalie came over and began watching. After a few minutes, she pulled up a chair next to her grandpa, captivated by the raw confession coming from her mother's mouth.

I went on to describe the pain I saw in her eyes—pain I had caused—and how my response to that pain led to real, positive, lasting change in my life. Watching my own reflections on this painful yet life-changing experience on the screen, coupled with the talk Natalie and I had shared on the beach earlier that night, I savored a new level of appreciation for the choice I'd made over eight years ago.

Looking back, I realized how easy it would have been to walk by the pain I saw in my child—to deny my part in it and to ignore the warning signs indicating change was desperately needed.

But I didn't take the easy path. Through God's grace, I didn't walk by.

I knelt down on the rice-covered floor and acknowledged what I saw, what I did, and perhaps most importantly, what I could do next.

In that moment, my decision to stop and respond to suffering had revealed just how far off course I'd gotten from the young dreamer who noticed and acted on behalf of the plight of all living creatures. In the frenzy of my overloaded agenda, I'd deemed it inefficient, wasteful, weak, and irresponsible to *pause* and *feel*. As damaging as that mindset was to my own well-being, it was even more debilitating to my children. How many times had my daughters cried, only to receive a harsh prompt to shake it off and just keep going? How often had I trivialized or minimized their worries because I didn't have the time to uncover what was happening underneath it all? How many emotional cues for support had I overlooked in my haste? Those were some really tough questions to ask myself, and it would have been easy to shut out those hard feelings.

Not this time, I told myself.

By learning to sit with my own feelings—especially the hard ones—I was advocating not only for my own well-being, but also guiding my daughters to advocate for theirs in a culture that glorifies powering through pain.

As I began carving out ten distraction-free minutes each morning to be still, set aside my worries, and listen to my innermost needs, healing words bubbled to the surface.

See flowers, not weeds.

Come as you are.

Today matters more than yesterday.

I am enough.

I wrote these mantras on sticky notes and posted them throughout the house. The bright yellow squares served as stop signs, reminding me to pause, check in with my heart, and respond with compassion, no matter how unpleasant the real feelings were. I found these mantras to be most helpful when I faced especially big feelings. When my environment was unstable and chaotic, rather than lashing out as I had in the past, I recited a mantra, accessing a place of peace inside myself. By practicing feeling peaceful each morning, I was able to channel this perspective when I, or those around me, needed it most. This led to another powerful mantra: *Let me be peace in the chaos.*

Don't get me wrong; this is not to say I've never had another emotional outburst, or that I consistently model healthy coping skills. I am human, and certain seasons of life can cause regression.

In fact, during one such season, I was battling an ongoing bladder infection, completing my second book, and managing end-of-the-school-year mayhem. In this depleted and overwhelmed state, I raised a casserole dish over my head and smashed it on the kitchen counter. I terrified Natalie, who happened to be in the kitchen at the time.

When I went to her room to apologize, I realized and admitted all at once that I was not taking care of my mind, body, spirit, and soul.

I'll never forget Natalie's response: *Are you drinking enough water, Mama? How many hours of sleep are you getting? Do you get your heart rate up when you exercise? Have you been outside today? I can make you some tea, Mama. Just sit and rest.*

At twelve years old, Natalie knew the importance of physical, emotional, and mental wellness, as well as some pretty sound self-care tactics to support it. I had modeled some of these practices, and others she'd improvised, but in that moment, she was being *my* guide.

Good Guides know they don't have to have all the answers, but they know when and how to rely on good resources to help them navigate hard times. Guides remind others to call on their own internal strengths and demonstrate how to trust that God is with us in our suffering. Furthermore, although Guides can falter, depending on how they handle their missteps, they can offer valuable examples that struggling, especially in a difficult season of life, is not something to be ashamed of—that this is what it means to be human. At times, we all need support. We all need to be reminded that life is not without struggles, challenges, or disappointment. It's better to come to terms with that fact than to ignore it, repress it, or deny it. Guides can be the ones to speak openly about the complexities of life, and by doing so, they can be the ones to arm others—especially young people—with the power of resilience.

Perhaps nothing is as complex as navigating the teenage years. Insecurity? Check. Peer pressure? Check. Too many expectations? Check. Teenage life has always been a source of stress and anxiety, but in the last decade, the number of American teens reporting "overwhelming anxiety" has surged. According to the National Institute of Mental Health, one-third of adolescents report feeling anxiety to a significant degree, and that percentage doubles in young adulthood. In a recent study by the American College Health Association, 62 percent of college students say they feel "overwhelming anxiety."[1]

---

1. Cited in Julie Mazziotta, "Teen Stress Is on the Rise: Why It's a Major Problem, and How You Can Help," *People* Magazine, May 14, 2018, https://people.com/health /teen-stress-rising-what-to-do/.

Kids today are under extreme pressure, and many either have little or feel little support. In addition to family, school, and work, they are maintaining online identities with "shareability" that spans a global stage and garners real-time feedback. The mental and emotional pressure created by these social media platforms can manifest an environment ripe with angst. While experts consider various potential sources of the angst, my speaking engagements and work with teens leads me to believe that this isn't just the latest incarnation of "the troubled teen years." Take a look at what young people have shared when I ask them to participate in the Index Card Exercise:

- *There's no time to be a kid; no time to just "be" and not "do."*
- *Why are such crazy awful things happening in our world? What did we do to deserve these terrible things?*
- *Parents assume our lives are a breeze when, in reality, we need to study, maintain friendships, and keep up with the expectations of basically everyone and everything.*
- *Parents need to feel comfortable talking to their kids; their kids need a role model to guide them.*
- *Parents need to stop blaming us when we get depressed or have anxiety and actually try to help us, because those things are prominent in today's youth, and people are turning a blind eye to it.*
- *I wish my parents understood that dance and school are very stressful, that—on top of homework and studying—they leave me no time to be a kid. Kids who do year-round sports deserve more credit for all that they handle.*
- *I wish there were more nice people in the world.*
- *Why can't the world be peaceful?*
- *Sympathy isn't always what we want. Listen. Be that shoulder to cry on. Don't say you understand. Everyone says that. That phrase is overused. If we need to scream, let us scream. Sympathy isn't always wanted.*

- *Parents need to be more aware of symptoms of mental illness like depression because it is spreading rapidly through teens.*
- *I wish adults would take care of the environment. It makes me so sad to see people destroying it.*
- *I wish parents would understand what we go through in our everyday lives in the twenty-first century is different from what they went through. I wish they could realize their job as parents in the twenty-first century is to help relieve the constant anxiety teenagers feel.*

While many of us can still remember the worries and stressors we experienced when we were young people, most would agree that there are far more external pressures and threats in our kids' world than the one we grew up in. It only takes one look at the news to feel angered, saddened, scared, and hopeless about the unstable world our kids must learn to navigate. Most adults are just trying to keep up with the latest threats, whether it's social media hazing tactics, the latest school shooting, or new household products kids are using to get high. Despite the overwhelming sense of risk everywhere we turn, we have to remember that our most important job is to be the safe haven, a respite from the worries young people feel. We cannot focus on thwarting every threat they might encounter, but we can empower our kids with awareness about and support for the complexities of the world they—and we—are living in.

Dr. Lisa Damour, author of *Under Pressure: Confronting the Epidemic of Stress and Anxiety in Girls*, states that the most powerful force for good in a teenager's life is a "caring, working relationship with at least one loving adult."[2] This relationship might be rooted in empathy and perspective or simply words of encouragement

---

2. Lisa Damour, qtd. in Deborah Farmer Kris, "How to Help Teenage Girls Reframe Anxiety and Strengthen Resilience," *Mind/Shift* (blog), *KQED News*, February 12, 2019, https://www.kqed.org/mindshift/52994/how-to-help-teenage-girls-reframe-anxiety-and-strengthen-resilience.

as they work through challenges—teaching them to instinctively rely on courage, not avoidance.

"Brave is a positive word—it's something we aspire to be," writes Damour. "Built into the word is the understanding that the person is scared and yet they are doing something anyway. Scared is here to stay. Anxiety is part of life. It's not our job to vanquish these feelings. It's our job to develop the resources we need to march forward anyway."[3]

In order to properly guide teens through these times, we must model healthy coping behavior. Keep in mind that the parts of the brain most vulnerable to stress are still maturing in teens, so coping strategies for stress and anxiety can manifest in both healthy (walking, exercising, talking) and unhealthy (escape, drugs, solitude) ways. These tactics, developed during the teen years, can become ingrained in the brain's circuitry as lifelong patterns, according to a recent research review in *Developmental Science Review*. The walking routine my parents instilled in me in grade school is one I still call upon today when I need to relieve stress.

While Natalie has adopted my walking practice, Avery's outlet is her music. It gives me hope to see that each of my daughters are developing healthy coping habits which will be available to them when they need them most.

Although it's hard to imagine our kids experiencing depression and anxiety to the point of feeling desperately unloved or unable to function, we must consider that this is a real possibility. Keeping these realities in mind provides additional motivation to serve as the Guides our kids need to help them rebound from virtually all forms of adversity. We can do this by . . .

- Teaching and modeling forms of healing, coping, and resilience-building.

---

3. Ibid.

- Acknowledging that pain is a part of life and allowing ourselves to both feel it (rather than repress or deny it) and let it fuel our momentum.
- Helping kids discover ways to "fill their cup" and recharge when life feels like too much.
- Countering the messages from modern media sources that suggest we should always feel good, that doing nothing is lazy and unproductive, and that we have to have everything figured out.
- Recognizing and managing our own fears, anger, and other negative emotions when we are interacting with our kids.
- Pointing out that we each possess internal strength, and we must learn how to tap into that when hardship hits.
- Being available.

In the pages ahead, we'll consider how to help young people become more resilient by applying three strategic concepts: *Overcoming*, *Relating*, and *Listening*.

In a world that looks for the quick fix, that prefers to numb the pain rather than do the work to heal, that resists the need to talk about hard things like mental health, we often walk right past ourselves and our loved ones in times of struggle. When we do, we forfeit the chance to connect, heal, and strengthen through a loving response.

But the truth is, there is
no heart too broken,
no issue too complicated,
no damage too severe,
no predicament too impossible,
no connection too severed
to be restored.
"I am here, take my hand," we'll say.

And then we'll walk side by side, training ourselves to stop
    for pain and suffering.
This is how we'll heal the world.
And find peace, connection, and strength in the process.

Life may be filled with adversity, but there is hope in knowing
we are prepared to guide so that our kids don't walk alone.

RESILIENCE THROUGH OVERCOMING

I was in the middle of wrapping Christmas presents when my
phone rang. The name of a beloved friend appeared on the screen.
I predicted she'd received the gift I'd sent, along with a letter of
encouragement. It was the kind of letter I would want to receive
in the midst of a steady stream of disappointment and dead ends.

When I said hello, I heard only muffled sobs.

After a few moments, my friend was able to say, "Thank you."
After that, months and months of heartache came pouring out—
some details of her life I knew, others I did not. I simply listened
as she unloaded the heavy burdens she'd been carrying.

"It's all a mess," my friend concluded. "I've lost so much, and
I feel like I've failed my kids."

I spoke softly but firmly, making a prediction about the future
that I had no idea how I knew; I just knew.

"Your kids may not appreciate or understand it now," I said,
"but mark my words: Someday they will be faced with a monumental challenge, and they will remember you in this exact
moment. They will remember how you managed to stand when
the whole world was pushing you down. And they will say to
themselves, 'That is what I am made of—courage, strength, faith,
resiliency, and love. My story isn't over.'"

My friend stopped crying.

The certainty in my voice astounded me, too.

How did I know this? How did I know that my friend's model of resilience today would be her children's foundation of strength in the future?

The question plagued me for several days as I thought about my friend's situation. It wasn't until my family celebrated the holidays with my parents in South Carolina that the pieces came together.

My dad was making his way down the beach access ramp, gripping his cane in one hand and the railing with the other.

Suddenly, I had a flashback to my high school graduation party. Perhaps it was because the day itself was a rite of passage, an acknowledgement of hard work and a celebration for the start of a new chapter (and new challenges) ahead, but something compelled my mom to blurt out an unusual request as my family prepared our dining room table for the festivities.

"Harry," my mom said, turning to my dad solemnly, "tell Rachel about the ramp."

I knew my dad had been stricken with polio at age eleven and that he'd been hospitalized for many months, unable to see his family. I knew he was told he would most likely never walk again, but I did not know about the ramp.

My dad set down the plate of crackers he was carrying and began to tell his story.

One day during my hospital stay, my physical therapists and doctor took me to a room where there was a long ramp with two railings on each side.

"We want to see if you can walk," they said.

Although I was only eleven, I knew that if a polio survivor could not walk on his own, the doctors would put a brace on the leg. They would wrap it, and the knee would never bend. The muscles would get weak, and the polio survivor would never walk again. I knew I did not want that to happen to me.

I said to my doctors, 'Don't wrap my leg. Let me try to walk the ramp.'

I wanted to try because I knew this would determine my destiny.

I dragged myself all the way down and back, leaning on the bars, using the strength of my upper body.

The hospital staff, looking amazed, said, "Well, maybe you can learn to walk."

I remember feeling so distraught when I heard my dad's story that I had to leave the room. I went into the kitchen and sobbed into a dishtowel. I remember hugging my dad before the party guests arrived, a silent acknowledgement that I was in awe of his strength and resiliency.

Little did I know my dad's story would come back to me at pivotal times in my life.

As a young special education teacher, I'd accepted a position teaching twelve elementary-age children who had been kicked out of multiple classrooms across the school district due to behavior problems. I arrived each day not knowing if I'd be spit on, cussed out, or clung to in desperation. As I sat in the associate principal's office one November morning, ready to quit, I remembered my father persevering to keep his body moving. Instead of turning in my resignation, I asked for help and remained with my students until the year's end.

My father's story helped me rise.

Years later, moving several states away from family and friends as a new mother took an emotional toll on me. I became severely depressed and barely avoided a head-on collision while driving distracted and sleep-deprived. I came home shaken but determined to get support. I got in touch with the local university and hired a college student to come to our home and stay with my daughters a few hours a week while I took walks by myself.

My father's story helped me rise.

When Avery and Natalie were four and seven years old, I realized I'd become someone I barely recognized—critical, joyless, and disconnected. My daughters were afraid of me, and Scott missed me. I fell to my knees on a deserted road while out for a run, praying for clarity to see how to take the next step toward changing the damaging course I was on before it was too late.

My father's story helped me rise.

Three years ago, I suffered a long bout of mysterious infections that caused severe pain and fatigue. Doctor after doctor neglected to find the source of the pain, but I continued to search for answers. Finally, a skilled urologist discovered a monstrous kidney stone that required two surgeries to remove.

My father's story helped me rise.

Two years ago, grief, exhaustion, and shame led me to believe my family would be better off without me. While staying in a hotel room in Canada, I considered permanently leaving this earth. But instead of taking the fire escape stairwell to the fiftieth floor, I reached for my phone and scrolled through my pictures. By spending time looking at the faces of Scott, my daughters, my parents, and my sister, I felt God's steadfast love willing me to hold on.

My father's story helped me rise.

In *The Secrets of Happy Families*, Bruce Feiler writes, "The single most important thing you can do for your family may be the simplest of all: develop a strong family narrative. The more children know about their family's history, the stronger their sense of control over their lives, the higher their self-esteem, and the more successfully they believe their families function. Create, refine, and retell the story of your family's positive moments and your ability to bounce back from the difficult ones. That act alone may increase the odds that your family will thrive for many generations to come."[4]

---

4. Bruce Feiler, "The Stories That Bind Us," *This Life* (blog), *New York Times*, March 15, 2013, https://www.nytimes.com/2013/03/17/fashion/the-family-stories-that-bind-us-this-life.html?pagewanted=all&_r=1&.

Having a model of resilience throughout my life motivated me to ask my almost-eighty-year-old dad to share his polio story with his granddaughters during that holiday gathering. On an unseasonably cold afternoon, Natalie and Avery sat in the condo, unaware that they were about to receive a priceless gift.

"I was the same age as you, Avery, when I contracted polio," my father began, looking at his youngest granddaughter.

As I listened to my dad, I felt certain his story of overcoming hardship would live on in my daughters and serve as inspiration to persevere when they need it most. Although the impact is yet to be seen, watching my dad share his story had an immediate impact on me. Right then and there, I decided I should be more forthcoming with my kids about my struggles, stumbles, and failings.

It was only a few days later, at the beginning of the new year, that I got the opportunity.

"Have you been crying?" Avery asked when she got home from school.

I'd had an emotional breakdown that afternoon. I felt scared and overwhelmed as I poured my heart into the final stages of launching my first online course. I thought about telling Avery I was fine, but instead, I gave her truth.

"Yes," I admitted. "I felt scared about something new I'm doing because it means being brave about painful experiences in my life in order to help other people. I stopped to breathe. I reminded myself that breaks are necessary in life, and when I did that, I cried. I feel more at peace now."

Avery hugged me. "We're Noticers, and we feel things deep in our hearts and brains. That makes us special."

As my daughter wrapped her arms around me, a whole new wave of relief washed over me. Parents are often led to believe that we have to be strong, that we must portray ourselves as invincible and all-knowing. But the truth is, the more human we are, the more likely we will be perceived as credible and relatable Guides with vital information worthy of following.

In the face of failure, shame, and embarrassment, in times of loss and rejection, in moments of pain and trauma, our kids will recall the moments they saw us struggle. But it won't be the struggle they will remember most; it will be the resilience, the effort, the refusal to give up and the willpower to keep trying. Our effort may have not been pretty, graceful, or anywhere near perfect, but we tried, and we didn't lose hope. We held on and made it to the other side.

My friend whose life was in such disarray several years ago is getting closer to the other side. Things have not been easy, nor have they gone as expected, but she now has a good job, a small home of her own, the love of her beautiful kids, and precious pups. She recently called to tell me her divorce would soon be final. Her voice didn't waver when she spoke, and there was no talk of failure or loss. In fact, I detected a newfound strength in my friend. She no longer focuses on where she's sliding; she focuses on where she's showing up. That type of shift is the building block of a strong family narrative, and it's one worth owning and passing on to those we love.

If things are far from where you want them to be,
do not be ashamed.
Instead, shift your focus.

Shift from, "I need to hide how badly I'm failing," to *"I'm showing them what I'm made of."*
Shift from, "This is not how it's supposed to be," to *"Watch me shine in the light of the unexpected."*
Shift from, "My beloveds shouldn't see me struggle," to *"These are the silver linings of my resilient soul."*
The strength you show in your current challenge will someday be the foundation on which your loved ones stand.

The strength you demonstrate today could be what lifts them on their darkest days.

How you love yourself through mistakes will likely be the way your children love themselves through their own mistakes.

How you collect yourself and move forward with courage and love will likely be the way your kids move forward with courage and love.

Maybe it will be a glance in the mirror, a photo on the nightstand, a family heirloom on their finger, or the lines in their palms that will halt the barrage of hopeless thoughts.

A voice of certainty from deep within will cut through the haze: *You are divinely designed—made of courage, strength, faith, resiliency, and love. Your story is not over.*

With shaking hands, your beloveds will grasp the railing and start making their way to the other side.

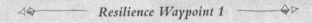

Resilience Waypoint 1

A UNIFYING FAMILY NARRATIVE

The most rewarding part of sharing my obstacles with my kids and having them share theirs with me is the message we are communicating: *We are in this together.* Just as Bruce Feiler described, "the story of your family's positive moments and your ability to bounce back . . . may increase the odds that your family will thrive for many generations to come."[5]

---

5. Bruce Feiler, "The Stories That Bind Us," *This Life* (blog), *New York Times*, March 15, 2013, https://www.nytimes.com/2013/03/17/fashion/the-family-stories-that-bind-us-this-life.html?pagewanted=all&_r=1&.

While there are many positives that can result from our honest admissions, we need to make a distinction between sharing in order to build a strong family narrative and placing an unnecessary burden on the shoulders of our kids.

Like it or not, life provides all of us with plenty of subject matter, including difficult experiences we've overcome or might still be struggling with—illness, death, loss, mental health, aging parents, divorce, addiction. Knowing how to put these difficulties in the proper context and when to bring them up will depend on several factors. Struggles are most appropriately shared when we have arrived at some conclusions, have a plan in place, have experienced healing, and when we are calm rather than emotionally distraught. Challenges should be shared at age-appropriate levels and not as a means of venting, gossiping, or unloading on the child. They should be shared with the emotional maturity and temperament of the child in mind. While my older daughter has an insatiable thirst for information and yearns for the difficult details, my other daughter has nightmares about sensitive subjects, so I keep this in mind when I decide how and what to share with each of them.

When I am directly in the midst of a struggle, having a hard time managing my emotions, and feel like I might lose control, I tell my kids this: "I'm having trouble talking right now, and I can't talk right now because I feel very frustrated."

If I am able, I might even briefly tell them why: "I am late for this doctor's appointment, and I feel stressed when I am running late," or "I am feeling really upset because I accidentally erased a fourth of the book I am writing" (true story), or "Speaking events make me anxious, but that just shows me how much I care and want to do a good job."

So that my kids are not left wondering how they should respond, I may say, "Thank you for giving me quiet right now while I calm down," or "What I could really use right now is your kindness and love."

Although I did not practice emotional regulation during my children's early years, failing to do so helped me understand how important it is for them to know *my struggle is not about them.* As I have uncovered specific factors that are emotional triggers for me, I have let my family know about them. Not only does this help me to have inner peace during the stressful situation, but my kids are prepared. For example, when I become lost while driving, my heart begins to race, and my brain is clouded by fear. When I say, "I am lost," Natalie offers assurances such as, "It's okay, Mom. We can ask for help," or "Let's pull over. We'll figure this out together."

Often, my daughters will come to me after I've experienced a setback to see how I am doing and ask if I'm feeling better. I believe this is another benefit of sharing our struggles in a healthy, responsible way. Not only does it model healthy coping skills for our children, but it gives them a chance to be empathetic. What a gift that will be to their friends, family members, and even to themselves in the future.

When sharing our struggles—whether small daily problems, heavy current issues, or struggles of the past—it is important to consider our delivery and tone as much as the words we say. This does not mean we shouldn't show emotion. Each time I told my children we were moving away from family and friends, I cried. But while I told them I was sad, I also said, "I believe there is a reason God is directing us to this place, and we're going to be okay because we have each other."

That last line, spoken many times throughout my life, is a critical piece to building a unifying family narrative: *We will stick together through thick and thin, and we are divinely equipped to handle whatever comes our way.*

RESILIENCE THROUGH RELATING

One day, while blogging, I linked back to a previous post in which I'd confessed to having suicidal thoughts. When one of my readers emailed and said, "Please forgive me; at the time, I didn't believe you," I understood.

I know what it's like to look at someone and think he or she couldn't possibly feel the depths of despair that you do. But then the person puts words to it, and you suddenly feel less alone. That's when skepticism turns to belief and despair turns to hope—you are not the only one.

The reader's words, in conjunction with the rise in youth suicide attempts researchers have observed in recent years,[6] sparked a mission in me. I set out to talk about the feelings no one wants to talk about, the feelings we want to pretend we don't have, the feelings that make us think there's something wrong with us.

I began these conversations close to home with my children, focusing on mental health. Depression touched my life from a young age, compelling me to prepare, equip, and inform my daughters in hopes that there would be no secrets between us.

I subscribe to the belief that knowledge is power, knowledge is armor, knowledge is love. Whenever a window opens for conversation about difficult topics, I muster up the courage to seize the opportunity and talk about this beautiful and often challenging life. My hope is that when one of my daughters encounters something beyond her frame of reference, she will not feel helpless or hopeless. She will be able to say to herself, *Mom and I talked about this.* I hope this sense of familiarity will feel like a light in the darkness.

As I've come to know and embrace my most authentic self,

---

6. According to the Centers for Disease Control and Prevention, suicide is the third-leading cause of death in young people between the ages of ten and twenty-four, resulting in about 4,600 lives lost in the U.S. each year.

I've discovered that Avery and I have more in common than I previously thought. Although our pace of life and levels of efficiency make us seem vastly different on the outside, we are eerily similar on the inside. We both feel deeply and experience life at a heightened level, often taking in more pain and heaviness than it seems a soul can bear. Because of this, I make it a point to routinely talk to her about mental health. Although Avery shies away from sensitive subject matters, song lyrics always open her up.

A song will play on the radio, and Avery will ask, "Is this about the singer's dad leaving?" or, "I think I know what 'unsteady' means in this song."

Avery took the death of Chester Bennington of *Linkin Park* especially hard. She'd been learning "One More Light" on her guitar shortly before he died by suicide.

"Is the person singing this song not here anymore?" she asked when the song "Iridescent" came on the radio.

After I said yes, a question she routinely asks came next.

"Depression runs in our family, doesn't it?"

It may sound odd, but I relish this question. It offers an opportunity to talk about our family history, the signs of depression, and how depression differs from just feeling sad. It offers us a chance to talk about what to do if we think we're depressed or someone we love is depressed.

Avery always seems satisfied with the discussion, with knowing, with gaining a better understanding of the genetic fabric within.

"Thank you, Mom," Avery always says, as if intuitively knowing these talks are not easy but crucial.

In addition to information, I've begun to give her tools I wish I'd had when anxiety gripped me in my younger days. Like me, when Avery is feeling stressed or worried, the feelings surface in vivid dreams and nightmares.

"I can't get the scary face out of my head," Avery said recently, when she came racing into my bedroom in the middle of the night. "When I close my eyes, that's all I see."

I ushered my daughter back to bed, and I told her about the file folders in my brain. I have one marked "Joy," where I've memorized moments of joy to refer to when I need to refocus negative thoughts. At the top of my Joy folder was a perfect moment to share with her.

"Remember going to the pet store next to the Hawaiian shave ice place? Remember that extra fluffy bunny you got to hold? Remember how he tickled your neck and made you laugh so hard?"

When I'd taken a photo of the moment to send to her grandma, I knew I would not need the picture to recall the sights and sounds of that delightful moment. It would be in my mind's Joy folder forever.

"Keep talking," my daughter said, still breathing heavily.

I flipped to another moment in my mental file folders and described the azure blue butterfly that followed me on a recent walk; I then flipped to the moment I felt the white sand of Siesta Key Beach beneath my feet and how it was surprisingly cool in the sun, unlike typical beach sand.

Around the fourth Joy moment I described, Avery's breathing returned to normal.

When Avery thanked me for helping her, a powerful thought came to mind: *Gratitude is not necessary, my precious child. These moments, this work of preparing you to survive and thrive in this difficult world, is my most important job as a parent.*

I want my child to have tools to help her overcome anxiety, images to flip to when darkness sets in, and a hand to hold when she thinks no one on earth could possibly feel the same way.

She will remember that I did.

And just knowing she is not the only one can be lifesaving.

When I learned of my dad's battle with depression in my

mid-twenties, it had a profound impact on me. Years after he came through the darkness, my mom told me how she urged him to get help. My dad checked into a residential treatment facility, where he stayed for several weeks. My mom undoubtedly saved my dad's life.

At the time, I remember thinking how hard that conversation must have been for my mom. But now I know there are certain moments in life when our personal comfort, our fear of rejection, our lack of having the right words must be put aside. There are certain conversations we simply must have with the people we love, even if we stumble in our delivery.

I've often wondered why my dad didn't tell me of his struggle himself. I suspect he thought I would think less of him.

Actually, it was quite the opposite.

I thought more of him.

And I thought more of myself.

My dad and I are eerily similar on the inside—in personality, temperament, work ethic, mannerisms, musical tastes, and empathy for others.

And I knew that if I had dark moments, I should reach out for help.

And I did.

And I do.

Never once have I thought, *There is something wrong with me.* Instead, I think, *This is part of my fiber, my genetic makeup, my family history. I'll talk to my parents about this; they will listen and will not judge me; they will understand because they've been here.*

My parents were, and still are, a safe haven for me, and that is what I wanted to be for my children. I prepared for the role by listening—it was the one thing I knew I could do well. No matter how badly I felt like I was failing in other areas, I could still listen, nod, understand, and hope that someday, my daughters would remember my listening face when they needed support.

During Avery's twelfth year, the result of my commitment to listening became evident. It had been a tumultuous spring for her—on top of usual puberty and peer issues were two unexpected x-rays revealing concerning conditions in her back and foot. Almost every night, I listened to her process her worries before she went to bed.

One night, Avery said, "One of my friends always comes to me for advice. Today, she said, 'Avery, how do you always know what to do?' And I told her it was because my mom is kind of like my therapist. She listens while I figure out what to do."

Here we were, in this tough situation for a young person to face, yet she had hope, confidence, and security for herself *and others* simply because she had not suffered alone. Although there were many times she and I didn't come to any definitive solutions, what mattered more is that we expressed hard things and sharpened our coping tools in the process. In this day and age, when so little of life is a clear yes or no, good or bad, this loving approach could quite possibly be the most effective way to equip our kids to navigate their complicated inner world, as well as the complexities of life.

◁❦———— *Resilience Waypoint 2* ————❦▷

LIFELINES THAT CONVEY BELIEF

Late one unforgettable spring night, I received a text message from a college friend. Within the first few words, I knew what I was about to read was critically important. My friend said she'd just had an unforgettable conversation with her teenage son over dinner. For three hours—yes, three hours—he described the pressures, worries, and dilemmas he carried around each day. My friend, a high school guidance counselor, offered this wisdom to me, words I knew were too powerful to keep to myself. With her permission, I share them here:

> There will come a time when our teens put down their phones, and we will have to be willing to listen. They'll want to talk to us about life, sex, drugs, alcohol, and friends, and we have to seize that moment to listen and not judge. If we are not listening, we will miss how they already have it figured out, how they are scared, how they are asking for our story, how they need our acceptance, guidance, and love. Because no matter how tough and independent they may appear, our kids need to know that they can talk to us and that we are listening. By listening, you might find they don't want to drink, or do drugs, or have sex, but they are scared, and what you say to them in your stunned, I-thought-we-were-just-having-dinner moment matters.

Although my friend said she grappled with how to respond, I believe she said exactly what her son needed to hear:

> You are amazing, my beautiful, fourteen-year-old young man. I'm proud that you don't want to drink or have sex or do drugs, and I honor how hard that is. I celebrate the choices you are making and the wisdom and strength you are displaying. I believe in you. You will get through this challenging time by continuing to stay true to who you are. And you won't have to go it alone. I am here for you always. We will get through this together.

At some point, we'll all have hard conversations with the young people we love, and we'll hear things that are difficult to take in.

In anticipation of that moment, it is wise to be prepared with a few lifelines—words that convey belief when our loved ones face difficult situations. Here are a few to get you started as you begin creating a list of your own.

You haven't gotten it yet, but you will. I'll never forget watching my daughter's confidence plummet as the material in a particular class got more and more difficult. "I will never get it," she said defeatedly. My response was: *"Yet . . .* you haven't gotten it *yet,* but you will." This response came from Dr. Carol Dweck, who coined the term "growth mindset"—the idea that we can grow our brain's capacity to learn and to solve problems.[7]

Often, kids assume that if they don't get a particular subject or task right away, then they are not cut out for it—they are not capable of learning it. This mindset is both damaging and paralyzing. When you see your loved ones buying into this misconception, it is helpful to point out that the brain is capable of growing, just like a muscle in the arm. And just because they don't have the concept down yet doesn't mean they won't get it eventually if they keep exercising/stretching their brain. The word "yet" leaves the door of possibility cracked open for success.

One mistake doesn't ruin the whole story. This is what my dear friend and psychotherapist Kerry Foreman said to me the morning after my darkest night, while I was in Canada. I'd put work before family, and the result was devastating. I felt so ashamed and disappointed in myself that I couldn't find hope. When I reached out to Kerry for support, her advice was to look at my intention. She wisely pointed out that although the result wasn't what I had hoped, my intention had been to do my best.

---

7. Carol Dweck, "The Power of Believing That You Can Improve," TED video, 10:21, November 2014, https://www.ted.com/talks/carol_dweck_the_power_of_believing_that_you_can_improve.

I hadn't even considered my intention, but it helped to consider it. Hope prevailed when Kerry said, "Don't let one piece of the story ruin the whole thing."

I use Kerry's phrase whenever young people in my life are feeling ashamed or embarrassed by a mistake or poor decision. When they consider making rash decisions because of the compounded pressure of a misstep, I remind them that each day, the story of their lives is being written. One mistake doesn't ruin the beautiful pages they've already written—and they have so much goodness yet to write.

You are not failing, you are preparing. When a friend reached out to tell me her struggling new business was going to have to close, she used the words, "I failed." I responded, not knowing the impact a slight change in perspective would have on my friend. A few months later, she reported that I'd helped her see how she could use her experience and story to inspire young people in her community who struggle with depression and isolation. This was my response that changed her outlook:

> I am 100 percent certain everything you did over the past year has prepared you for what is coming next. Even though we don't know what is next, it is hopeful and helpful to anticipate that something important is coming. Here is what I envision:
>
> On a momentous day in your future, an unexpected role will present itself. It might look scary, intimidating, difficult, or impossible, but to you, it will feel like a possibility. Here is where you come in. You will walk right up to that door and know exactly what to do and say. In a voice brave and strong, you'll deliver a message no one else can deliver. You will provide hope where there

is none. Why? Because of where you are today. Because of the courageous choice you are making to let go, give it time, and accept change so that you are available for *what is next.*

So you see, you are not failing, you are *preparing—* and there is a BIG difference.

It's the difference between seeing what you wish you could've done and what you *did* do and *will* do.

It's the difference between seeing what you can no longer do and what you can do *now.*

It's the difference between seeing wasted resources and experiences gained.

It's the difference between seeing who you think you disappointed and to whom you will bring hope.

In the coming days, may you experience a powerful perspective shift: from failure to preparation.

Helping our kids shift their focus from how they think a situation *should have* turned out to what it's preparing them for *next* opens the door to hope and possibility, inspiring them to examine how their purpose might be found somewhere in the struggle.

It's not too late to turn things around. It's easy to miss the gift that is today when disappointment, shame, failure, or loss distorts our view. Be that person who reminds a discouraged young person of this hopeful truth: *You are never too far gone to come back. You are never too broken to be made whole. It's never too late to make changes. It's never too late to begin again. Today matters more than yesterday. Who you are becoming matters more than where you are and how fast you're getting there.*

RESILIENCE THROUGH LISTENING

On an ordinary Tuesday night, while we gathered around the dinner table as a family, Avery casually told us she'd hid in the school's walk-in freezer with her class during a Code Red drill.

This was not a routine fire drill or a tornado siren warning of inclement weather. It was practice for a Code Red threat, which meant there was an active shooter in the school, and thus, imminent danger. It took a moment to process the words I'd just heard and the troubling image produced in my mind, but as I did, reality hit me hard. This is our new normal.

As I composed my thoughts, I wondered if I should downplay the occurrence to avoid fueling a sense of fear about an environment my child should feel comfortable learning in—a place she spends nearly as much time in as our home. While it would have been easier to skim the surface and change the subject, I knew this was an opportunity to lean in, so I used what I'd learned from the experts. I asked open-ended questions so my daughter could take the lead, showing me where she needed more information and how she felt about the situation. Her responses indicated there was no reason to create further angst by adding my own emotional reaction to the situation.

The topic came up again a few days later as our family prayed for the seventeen fatally wounded students and staff and countless others who were physically injured and emotionally scarred by the mass shooting at the hands of an expelled classmate at Marjory Stoneman Douglas High School in Parkland, Florida.[8]

I'd intentionally given myself time to take in the news reports and release my emotions before our family sat down at the table. Through the work of Sandy Blackard, I've become aware that my emotions can cause me to miss important details about difficult

---

8. Elizabeth Chuck, Alex Johnson, and Corky Siemaszko, "17 Killed in Mass Shooting at High School in Parkland, Florida," February 14, 2019, NBC News, https://www.nbc news.com/news/us-news/police-respond-shooting-parkland-florida-high-school-n848101.

situations my kids are facing and influence how they experience them. In order to support young people and remain open to *their* solutions, Sandy encourages adults to step from sympathy (*feeling* what the young person is feeling) into empathy (*understanding* what the young person is feeling and thinking). Instead of offering advice, attempting to understand their child's point of view on the situation allows the adult to play the more important role of a supportive coach, helping kids figure out their own solutions.

Once again, it was Avery who was most vocal about what the school was doing to prepare students and staff should an armed attacker enter the building. She reiterated what she would do if she were in the bathroom when a Code Red sounded. The fact that it was the second time she had brought up the possibility of being separated from her class when the alarm sounded indicated that was her biggest concern. Our family talked through the Active Shooter Response protocol of run-hide-fight. The three-pronged approach has been endorsed by the U.S. Department of Homeland Security since 2012 as part of a public safety campaign. The official DHS guidance is to run if possible; quietly hide, ideally in a place that can be locked if fleeing is not possible; and fight only as "an absolute last resort."[9]

After dinner, my daughters did homework upstairs while Scott and I watched the news reports about the Parkland shooting. Although I could easily have sat transfixed for hours, taking in the horrific details as they emerged, I turned off the television. My instincts told me my time would be better spent with my daughters.

First, I went to Avery's room. When I told her I'd been watching the news about the shooting, Avery's response indicated she didn't want to talk about it. I took her lead and sat quietly beside her. That's when she said, "I helped someone crying today

9. Jonathan Allen and Joseph Ax, "Run? Hide? Fight? Lockdown? Two U.S. School Shootings Highlight Differing Responses," *Reuters*, May 8, 2019, https://www.reuters.com /article/us-colorado-shooting-run-hide-fight/run-hide-fight-lockdown-two-us-school -shootings-highlight-differing-responses-idUSKCN1SE2LE.

on the playground. I didn't know her name, but she's in my grade. I went over and sat with her. She didn't want to tell me what was wrong, but she wanted me to stay, so that's what I did."

"Do you think you helped her?" I asked.

"Yes, because she stopped crying, and she smiled. I still don't know what was wrong, but sometimes just knowing you are not alone makes things better."

I kissed my child's forehead and thanked her for using her heart and her presence to help someone.

I then went to Natalie's room. She had not said much about the shooting. I figured since it did not directly impact her life, it was not on her radar.

I could not have been more mistaken.

"Will you lie down with me?" Natalie said. I hadn't heard that request in a while. With my arms around her, I waited quietly to see what might come.

What came was more information than even I knew about the shooting.

What came were details from a video taken by a student in one of the classrooms.

What came was a plan of what she would do in such a situation and how she would contact me if she didn't have a phone.

What came was a conversation about "weird vibes" she gets from two classmates.

What came was a promise to report any social media posts made by classmates that make her feel concerned.

What came was talk of the benefits of therapy and counseling. She said, "Everyone needs someone who will just listen to them sometimes."

All at once, I realized that both of my daughters, in their own unique ways, needed to talk through what they were seeing, hearing, and experiencing.

All at once, I realized that both of my children had good

instincts about keeping themselves safe that I could affirm and strengthen through reoccurring talks.

All at once, I realized that both of my children knew the vital importance—the life-saving potential—of listening.

For parents to listen to children.

For kids to listen to each other.

While there is no set protocol for talking to young people about such frightful facts of life, I believe there are key elements to actively listening during these conversations in order to create space for deep, honest, and effective communication. Offering undivided attention is a rare and priceless gift in today's culture.

It is asking hard questions and then sitting still to hear the response.

It is turning off the television and leaving the phone in another room.

It is lying beside your loved one until the words come.

It is hearing things that are hard to hear.

It is not assuming everything is fine just because your loved one doesn't have much to say.

It is being available, not just in the wake of tragedy but every day, so that a foundation is already in place when trouble arises and support is needed.

Before leaving my daughter's room, I wanted to shift the focus to something positive. I remembered that Natalie had spent the weekend baking eleven mini cherry pies from scratch, putting them into little brown boxes with ribbon, and delivering them to friends on Valentine's Day.

"Tell me how your friends liked their mini cherry pies," I said.

Natalie reported that all the girls loved the pies, but one friend was clearly moved by the gesture.

"My friend said no one had ever done anything like that for her," Natalie said quietly. "She shared some really hard things that are going on with her family. I think she felt better after we talked. I'm so glad I baked those pies."

And just when I thought I couldn't absorb any more information on such a hard and tragic day, Natalie provided the most beautiful piece of all: *There is still so much to experience in life that we must not take the safe route out of fear.*

It can be excruciatingly painful to send our loved ones off to school, onto the field, off to college or other unknown terrain when all we want to do is protect them from the worst parts of life. At times, the world can feel incredibly unsafe and scary, and not just the world we see on television each night, but the one that meets us each morning whether we're ready or not. There are firsts we must get through; there are hurtful people who intimidate and bully; there are tough situations with no easy answers; there are hardships and heavy burdens. It is not uncommon for our loved ones to lay their fears before us and for us to feel helpless. But let us not forget there is something powerful we can do to ease those fears.

Listen.

Just listen.

Our undivided attention not only has the power to ease someone else's fear, it can also bolster hope by laying a path for healing—one tended heart at a time.

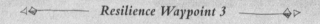
Resilience Waypoint 3

SIXTY-SECOND BREATHER

While my daughters and I were visiting my parents in Florida, I didn't expect to find a powerful stress-relief strategy in the pages of a *Family Circle* magazine on their coffee table. Since then, this strategy has enhanced our family's ability to accept uncomfortable feelings that arise during moments of fear, rejection, and instability.

It was the initial line of this collaborative article with no byline that caught my attention: "If meditation came in the form of a pill, it would be the best-selling drug on the market," Suze Yalof Schwartz, CEO and founder of Unplug Meditation was quoted as saying. "It gives you the opportunity to delete stress on demand and puts everything in perspective."[10]

I continued reading and was encouraged by three surprising points:

- A daily meditation practice—even just sixty seconds—has scientifically proven benefits such as lowered blood pressure, decreased depression and anxiety, and increased focus, memory, and productivity.
- A still mind is not required. Leonard Perlmutter, founder and director of the American Meditation Institute said, "Meditation is not meant to eliminate thoughts. It simply teaches you to direct the mind's mental traffic."
- Meditation can happen anywhere. "When you close your eyes, slow down your breath and get present, you're meditating," said Yalof Schwartz, which she stated could be done even while riding the subway or standing in line.

I'd often been curious about meditation, but it always seemed so elusive and out of reach to me, someone who had tied her self-worth to her productivity level for so long. For the first time, I had hope that maybe I could meditate. I marked the magazine page, but I knew I would not forget the words I'd read.

When I started taking what I called a "sixty-second breather," I noticed an emerging pattern. After I read or watched

---

10. "Take Time for Meditation," *Family Circle Magazine*, March 2018, 18.

distressing news reports or when I sat down to open my email or messaging inboxes, I often felt overwhelmed and stressed. I began using that stress as a cue to close my eyes and focus on a single point for one minute. As the article suggested, I closed my eyes, and then focused on my breath, a calming phrase, a sound, or an object. That's it.

One afternoon during that same visit to my parents', both of my daughters were expressing worry about future events. One daughter was scheduled to babysit for two young children and, in the wake of the Parkland School shooting, was feeling afraid. My other daughter had discovered that a missing assignment in one of her classes was affecting her overall grade, and she couldn't get it off her mind.

Seeing the worry in my daughters' faces, I invited them to try the sixty-second breather I had been using. I repeated a convincing line from the article suggesting the practice could "produce an instant sense of calm."

After a bit of reluctance, they agreed to try. The result was so positive that over the course of our five-day visit in Florida, my daughters and I used the meditation practice multiple times.

What I noticed most was a visible difference in anxiety levels upon our trip home—less angst about airport security, school assignments, appearance, and upcoming events, like the babysitting job. I wasn't sure there was a connection, but the difference felt like a stabilizer during stressful times.

In what can only be explained as divine intervention, there was a package waiting for us when we got home. A dear reader of my blog had sent each of us a necklace that had a tiny map of the entire world. "Go be love," the beautiful medallion read.

Natalie walked through the kitchen and immediately picked

up one of the necklaces and asked where it came from. I told her about this particular woman's "Love Mission." In order to bring healing to a broken and isolating time in her life, she was reaching out to people on her gratitude list.

"This is pretty amazing, considering I just decided to apply for the African Road Learning Trip to Rwanda," Natalie said.

As Natalie undid the clasp to put on the necklace, she said something that astounded me: "Remember how you said an object can be a focus point in the sixty-second breather? I will be able to hold this charm throughout the day and remember my purpose when life's pressures start getting to me."

Natalie has continued practicing the sixty-second breather along with other healthy coping techniques associated with music and exercise, but it takes effort and self-discipline. Learning to sit with their most uncomfortable feelings does not come naturally to our children—goodness knows, it does not come naturally to many adults! It is something we must practice, and we can do it together.

First, we become aware. We learn to recognize when fear and anxiety are speaking and, rather than rejecting ourselves and our uncomfortable feelings, we sit with them. This is a vastly different message than the one the world glorifies, and if our kids don't hear it from us, they are not likely to hear it anywhere. The message, which can be spoken but is best lived out, is this:

It's necessary to get quiet.

It's necessary to be still.

It's necessary to surrender.

It's necessary to turn off the world and listen to the heart.

Even when the world is off-kilter, we have the ability to restore balance within ourselves.

Balance excessive information with thoughtful introspection.

Balance mindless talking with attentive listening.

Balance frenzied doing with prayerful being.

Balance biased opinions with heart-held beliefs.

Balance the superficial and fleeting with the deep and enduring.

The simple act of catching ourselves and pausing in these moments to connect our mind and body to our heart is vital for our personal—and, I dare say, global—healing. Fortunately, this act of holding our hearts in meditation is much less elusive than we've been led to believe. It's actually as simple as closing our eyes and focusing on the sound of our own breath. This is when we each allow our own heart to become a map, guiding our purpose and giving us definitive direction to find answers to hard questions.

What is this situation trying to teach me?

What is my purpose here?

How can I turn this into an opportunity for growth?

Teaching our kids to use their hearts as their guides can help them find their way out of the dark, without losing themselves along the way.

LIVE LOVE NOW REFLECTION: THE STEADY HAND OF LOVE

I Know Someone

I know someone going through a hard time.
He's irritable, overreactive, and difficult to be around.
That's grief talking, I remind myself,
And my love expands like an umbrella in a downpour.

I know someone going through a hard time.
She's moody and dramatic.
That's teen angst talking, I remind myself,
And my love settles and steadies like a faithful friend.

I know someone going through a hard time.
She's emotional, fidgety, and anxious.
That's fear talking, I remind myself,
And my love whispers to her like a calming prayer.

I know someone going through a hard time.
He's self-critical and unable to sleep.
That's anxiety talking, I remind myself,
And my love supports him like a great oak tree.

I know someone going through a hard time.
She's awkward and sassy.
That's hormones talking, I remind myself,
And my love endures like a worn pair of blue jeans.

I know someone going through a hard time.
He's defensive and angry.
That's depression talking, I remind myself.
And my love breaks through the clouds and warms his face.

It's not easy to respond when I want to retreat,
To forgive when I want to freak out,
To bite my tongue when I want to bite back.

But when you're going through a hard time, you feel shaky.
You feel weak in the knees.
You feel like you could blow away in the wind.
You feel like you're suspended in a place you don't want to be.

That's why a steady hand to ground you is especially helpful during
these times.

I know because that was me at certain points in my life,
Suspended in darkness.
I was anxious, overreactive, defensive, and moody.
But I was never alone.
Thank God, I was never alone.
Being not-alone is what brought me back.
Love's steady hand helped me regain my footing
So I could see my trial was temporary,
That my failings did not define me,
That my story was not over.

So when I see my loved ones going through a hard time, I do the
one thing I know helps:
I throw my weight behind them.
With feet firmly planted, I stay close.
"We'll get through this," I remind them as I remind myself.
Because it's easy to forget hard times are temporary and our failings
don't define us.

If we can just hang on to the steady hand of love, we'll find our
footing once again.

Let's be the steady hand of love for someone today.

Let's remember our stories are not over.

Let no one walk alone.

REFLECTION QUESTIONS

1. The pressure to constantly *do*, to be active and productive, puts stress on everyone in the family. When was the last time you spoke to the young person in your life about his or her schedule? Is there something he or she would like to stop doing? Is there a way to simplify and allow for some downtime and freedom to play?

2. Briefly reflect on your interactions with the young people in your life over the last few days. What have been your responses when they expressed negative emotions, pain, or worry? How do you feel about your responses? Is there anything you would like to do differently in the week ahead?

3. What are your go-to coping strategies when you feel stressed, depressed, overwhelmed, or sad? Do you ever share your struggles with the young person in your life, as well as what you did or are going to do about it? How might you build a strong family narrative about how to handle such issues in the upcoming weeks and months?

4. In what ways do you make yourself available to listen when the young person in your life wants to talk?

5. What is one of your favorite belief statements or lifelines to say when the young person in your life is facing tough times?

6. Describe how you took a painful experience and transformed it into purpose. If nothing comes to mind, consider a past or current pain from your life that you could "put work boots on . . . send out into the world . . . and give a job," as Laura Parrott Perry says.[11] What might that look like?

---

11. Laura Parrott Perry, "Freedom Song," *Laura Parrott Perry* (blog), August 16, 2019, https://lauraparrottperry.com/freedom-song/.

CHAPTER 6

NOT ENOUGH

Stop asking: Am I good enough?
Ask only
Am I showing up
with love?

Life is not a straight line
it's a downpour of gifts, please—
hold out your hand.

—Julia Fehrenbacher, "Hold Out Your Hand"

I don't always remember dates, but I do remember faces, images, emotions, and songs. This probably explains why I've always used photos to motivate myself.

When my children were young, the photo I kept inside my kitchen cabinet to motivate me had been taken a couple of years after I graduated from college, during a trip to Seattle with my mom and sister. As we set out in my sister's Honda Accord to take a ferry to Bainbridge Island, I can faintly recall 4 Non Blondes playing in the background, but more notably, a feeling of emptiness in my stomach that was becoming more frequent. My mom had expressed concern about my lack of appetite at breakfast. I got defensive and pushed her—and the pain—away. A few hours later, the three of us stood on the pier, asking a stranger to take our photo. *That* photo, showing me with a few pieces of hair tucked away from my face with butterfly clips—and wearing my smallest size ever—wasn't just a memento from our trip; it was a trophy.

When I got home from Seattle, I printed the photo, displaying it inside the most frequently opened kitchen cabinet of the starter home Scott and I bought shortly after our wedding. Even though I could still sense all the turmoil behind the radiant smile and flat stomach every time I looked at the photo, it reminded me that keeping that size was my goal, even as I raised my babies.

Throughout the years, I perpetually felt like I was falling short of the girl in the photo, but it never hurt quite as much as it did one New Year's Eve. Although I'd moved four times since I printed the photo, it always took its rightful place in the kitchen cabinet. It was there that night as I went to retrieve a snack for Avery before our family left for a party. While reaching for the bag of Goldfish crackers, my eyes lingered on my goal image. Looking down at myself, I did a before-and-after comparison. Cloaked in inadequacy, I responded unlovingly to Scott when he said I looked beautiful in my off-the-shoulder black dress. Minutes later, I responded ungratefully to my family when they presented me with a new camera. I insisted we take an unreasonable number of photos, determined to get the "perfect" shot. If you looked closely at the photo, you could see tears on the cheeks of my daughters, who were trying so hard to get it right.

I don't remember dates, but I can tell you what pajamas I was wearing and which room I was standing in when Scott tried to talk to me about his concern over the pace I was trying to maintain, stretching myself to the point of exhaustion and giving so much of myself that I had nothing left for the people who really mattered.

"We have a serious problem," Scott said, worried.

I'd noticed he said *we*, but I knew he meant *me*—*I* had a serious problem.

I remember thinking, *You have no idea.*

The pressure within was killing me. And I was certain it *would* eventually cause an early death. Although I never dared speak my thoughts aloud, I feared I would not see my young daughters graduate from high school. The pressure I was putting on myself to achieve perfection at any cost was causing me to take dangerous risks and unhealthy shortcuts.

I don't remember dates, but I remember the day I started posting love notes from my children on walls, doors, and bathroom mirrors. It was an act of desperation—a way of halting my ever-moving body and brain, grounding me for one glorious moment in the present so I could breathe.

The infamous snack cupboard became so full of love notes that I eventually had to cover up the girl—the girl who looked radiant and strong on the outside but was dimming and crumbling on the inside.

Backwards letters, an army of hearts, and faithful devotion brought a wave of relief each time I opened the cabinet. Despite how badly I felt I was missing the mark in most areas of my life, those notes provided tangible proof that I mattered and that my life had a purpose far beyond external variables. The notes were a form of validation that directly challenged the feelings of inadequacy produced by the picture in the girl who ran the extra mile but had no direction. The notes pointed me toward my children, and I could see them clearly . . .

Ready and waiting for me to love them—just as they were.

Ready and waiting to love me back—just as I was.

The love notes motivated me in ways the photo never could.

The loves notes filled me with peace I'd forgotten existed.

The love notes validated who I was as a child of God, created with a unique and glorious purpose.

When my daughters hugged me, I heard a divine whisper:

Don't get ahead of yourself—stay right here.

Don't get lost in the past—stay right here.

Love in the moment.

This is where life is.

I'd heard that message somewhere before. I wracked my brain until I remembered. I was in college, the first time I truly remember crumbling under the weight of pressure. My insecurity surged during my junior year, when I stepped onto the tennis court. My coach had placed me in the #1 singles position on the team, and my opponents were exceptionally tough. I felt completely out of my league and doubted my abilities; I considered giving up.

About midway through the season, an iridescent blue butterfly crossed the court during a match against DePauw University. Although my opponent was waiting on me to serve, I was awed and paused to watch the butterfly flitter around my head. Like a winged prayer, it spoke to me:

Don't get ahead of yourself—stay right here.

Don't get lost in the past—stay right here.

Love in the moment.

This is where life is.

Whether the match resulted in a win or a loss, I don't remember. But spotting a butterfly became my goal for the rest of the season and the final season of my college tennis career. I saw more butterflies during that period than I had in my entire life up to that time, and the reason was simple: *I chose to look for them.*

I don't remember dates, but I remember being in the middle of pouring cereal for my daughters when two pressing questions came to mind. I began rummaging through the kitchen drawers, frantically looking for something on which to write. Settling on the back of an oversized envelope, I wrote the following, as if my very life depended on it:

What if, instead of rushing through the minutiae of your daily life, you occasionally paused and offered your presence?

What if you turned away from the distractions that monopolize your time and attention and grasped the sacred moments passing you by?

I knew with certainty that those words were not just for me; they were to be shared with others. I'd just completed my teaching certification renewal process and was considering applying for a special education position in our new state. Sitting on the counter, just inches away from the envelope, was a book my sister had sent me on how to start a blog. Nearly all my life, Rebecca had known about my abandoned dream of being an author, so when blogging became all the rage, she encouraged me to try.

And so I did.

Combing through the notebooks I'd been writing in when my young daughters slept, I found raw, honest, hopeful admissions and tiny triumphs; words I thought might hold the power to make others feel less alone in their struggles. The blogging experts claimed there was a recipe for success: keep posts to eight hundred words or less, stick with a consistent posting schedule so your readers know what to expect, stay relevant by talking about current events, and garner X amount of followers within three months—if you don't, you're doing it wrong.

For the first time in decades, I chose to reject other people's standards for success and let my heart be my guide. Where others were aiming for followers, I wanted to build a community. Where others were showcasing their highlight reels, I wanted to bare my scars. Where others promoted their strengths, I wanted to be honest about my weaknesses. Where others deemed themselves experts, I wanted to be vulnerable, show honest and sometimes slow progress toward growth, and walk hand in hand with my readers. My organic, open-hearted approach was hardly the recommended method to build a brand or a platform, but God's divine whisper urged me to forge a new path, assuring me I would never walk alone.

The first year of blogging was not easy. My hands shook every time I posted my vulnerable insights for the world to read. Fear of rejection, lack of monetary compensation, and criticism of my writing and parenting might have led some to deem my endeavor a failure.

Yet I felt successful.

Why? Because my measure of success was this: to touch *one* life with each story I wrote. Just one.

Each time I received a message indicating my words had given someone hope and direction, I wept. I realized that by making others feel seen and heard through my writing, I could live out the kind of legacy I'd always wanted to leave.

Eight years and four published books later, my goal remains unchanged. I'm quite certain many social media gurus would tell you I could be doing so much more, but my response to them would be this: *Is there anything more important than using one's gifts to touch another person's life?*

I believe we can all choose to forge our own path and create our own definition of success. For this reason, I never focus on how-tos when I am asked to speak to students about becoming an author. What's more important than the ins and outs of a career is the story of how one flawed, fearful person got there. In my presentations, I always talk about the rejections, the doubts, the hard falls, the long days, and the sleepless nights. Through what can only be explained as divine guidance, I've begun to receive invitations to go back into the classroom, only this time not as a teacher, but as a guest speaker who uses her experiences to affirm young people for who they are right now: experts about their own unique attributes and truths.

I often share a photo with the students. It's not the emaciated, desperate young adult version of me I mentioned before, but instead a photo I call "my Dreamer girl," the girl who, at age eight, had nothing but my best interests and most authentic self at heart. What the students don't know is that this photo now hangs on the inside of my cupboard door at home. Unlike her predecessor, who fueled my insecurities, this girl motivates me to live a life of peace, purpose, and fulfilment.

After my most recent school visit, I received an email from a fourteen-year-old student. She wrote, "You may not have been able to tell, but you made a difference to a lot of kids, especially me. My parents want me to be something I'm not. I feel pressure all the time—I can't tell if it's coming from inside or outside, but it never lets up. You helped me see I don't have to live that way."

This young woman's message echoes the feedback I've received after using the Index Card Exercise in dozens of other schools. The students' handwritten responses reflect their yearning for support, guidance, trust, and acceptance from adults as they pursue their own worthwhile goals.

- *I wish my parents listened to my side of the story and didn't put so much pressure on me in everything, especially school.*
- *We have no idea what we want in life. Careers and hopes for our lives bounce around in our heads. They change weekly. We're kids. We have dreams but may not know how to achieve them yet. Adults need to allow us to dream without it being a big deal.*
- *We have to do what we feel in our hearts because a world without happiness isn't a world that is worth living in.*
- *I want people to believe in me and my dreams and not put me down when I need to be pulled up.*
- *My parents live through me; they don't ask me what I want. They say it's so I can be someone, but they always say, "I just need YOU to . . ."*

- *The educational system does not set us up to learn. It sets us up to memorize . . . and fail.*
- *I once missed a lot of school due to an illness. I got bogged down trying to catch up. I couldn't catch up and developed anxiety.*
- *Just because I am not good in one subject does not mean I am not smart.*
- *If I don't know what I want to do or be in life, will I have a bad one?*
- *It often feels like we have to pretend or enjoy something we really don't enjoy. It always seems like there is some kind of pressure on us, whether it be school, parents, or peers.*
- *Grades do not define us.*

The sentiments on the cards echo the heartbreaking question psychologist Katie Hurley hears on a daily basis from her young clients: *When will I ever be good enough?*

Our culture is so desperate to get ahead that we are leaving the most important things behind—joy, connection, integrity, truth, purpose, peace—and our kids are suffering for it. During a time in their lives when they need freedom to make mistakes and explore their inner and outer worlds, they are living a test of endurance, a checklist life, an insatiable pursuit in which taking a breather puts them out of the race.

Living in an age that is obsessed with rank, achievement, and external approval is stressful enough as it is, but for some young people, the stress is compounded by pressure to fulfill their parents' dreams or unrealistically high expectations. When grades, test scores, and trophies become more important than well-being and development, the results can be devastating. Sleep deprivation, eating disorders, excessive worrying, cheating, burnout, loss of interest in hobbies, or withdrawing from friends and family are all consequences of excess pressure.[1]

---

1. Jaime Budzienski, "The Effects of Academic Parental Pressure on Kids," *The Bump*, https://living.thebump.com/effects-academic-parental-pressure-kids-10380.html.

We know it is counterproductive to work for something you don't choose yourself; we know it is demoralizing to try to be someone or something you're not. Pressure to achieve detaches our kids from the core of who they are. It prevents them from hearing that faint internal voice that reveals their deepest, most heartfelt needs. Pressuring our kids to meet unrealistic expectations or to fulfill our own unmet dreams sets them up for failure and undermines their self-worth and self-confidence. Inevitably, their chance at long-term joy and fulfillment is sabotaged. In his book, *The Road to Character*, David Brooks explains the tragic consequences of a lifetime spent living for achievement: "Years pass and the deepest parts of yourself go unexplored and unstructured. . . . You live with an unconscious boredom, not really loving, not really attached to the moral purposes that give life its worth. . . . A humiliating gap opens up between your actual self and your desired self."[2]

As our kids "become" right before our eyes, it is vital that we choose to listen and guide them while *they* make internal shifts. We must encourage them to take ownership of their stories, uncover what's meaningful to them, and understand their full potential. This process will eventually lead to the development of the most powerful source of guidance they'll need—their own hearts.

Researcher and developmental psychologist Dr. Marilyn Price-Mitchell, who created a positive youth development framework called The Compass Advantage, extends this powerful invitation:

> It's time to look beyond external measurements to the internal abilities that help children and teens learn to successfully pilot their own healthy and productive lives. . . . Successful kids are not driven by external accomplishments alone.

---

2. David Brooks, "The Moral Bucket List," *New York Times*, April 11, 2015, https://www.nytimes.com/2015/04/12/opinion/sunday/david-brooks-the-moral-bucket-list.html.

In fact, they are inspired to perform to their highest potential when they are driven by their own internal compasses.[3]

In our roles as Guides, we can positively influence the development of young people's internal compasses by our actions and words. As we begin to live more aligned with our own true essence, we establish a safe, spacious, nurturing environment in which our kids can seek their purpose. Unlike the perfection-demanding, externally-focused culture in which we live, these conditions empower, inspire, motivate, and connect. We foster these conditions by:

- dialing back the focus on academic achievement
- broadening our definition of success to include effort and growth over achievement and accolades
- developing as individuals apart from our kids
- focusing on today rather than on the future
- setting realistic expectations
- accepting that our children's life pursuits might be different from their peers'
- asking questions that give young people a chance to express their thoughts, hopes, and dreams openly and honestly

In the pages ahead, we'll consider how to help young people realize the value of their full human potential through these three strategies: *Discovery, Affirmation,* and *Knowledge.*

More than likely, our culture and educational system will never stop pointing our kids to a narrow path of success—an unending and unhealthy pursuit to *be* more and *do* more. But we have the opportunity to forge a path to worthiness—from seeking external validation to cultivating inner transformation. Each time

---

3. Marilyn Price-Mitchell, PhD, "Successful Kids Need 8 Core Abilities: How to Parent with Purpose," *Roots of Action* (website), September 12, 2016, https://www.rootsofaction.com/successful-kids/.

we see new habits immerging, positive character traits forming, independence blooming, courage showing, let's pause and celebrate. Like a vibrant butterfly crossing your path, noticing the presence of such glorious development will inspire young hearts in ways extreme pressure never could.

WORTHINESS THROUGH DISCOVERY

Within the first few minutes of the parent orientation meeting, I knew I was in emotionally triggering territory. In a matter of forty-five minutes, I repeatedly heard the words *GPA*, *college visits*, *scholarships*, *tutoring*, *dual credit courses*, and *online grade portal* more times than I could count. It was no surprise I came home feeling clingy and controlling, filled with an urge to micromanage every detail of my soon-to-be high schooler's academic progress. All at once, it felt like so much was riding on her decisions and her achievements that there was no room for even one misstep.

Aware that this was not a healthy feeling, I knew I'd need to turn to some trusted sources to calm my angst and enlighten me. As fate would have it, later that day I stumbled on an article written by Jessica Lahey, author of *The Gift of Failure*. The fact that I felt challenged while reading her words indicated it was a message I needed to receive.

In the article, Jessica describes an informal survey she takes when speaking to high school students nationwide. After asking them to close their eyes, she says the following statements:

Raise your hand if you get paid cash money for good grades.

Raise your hand if you get any material thing in exchange for grades.

And then Jessica gives a third prompt, which she prefaces by saying, "This one's tougher to answer and requires thoughtful and honest reflection."

Raise your hand if you truly believe your parents love you more when you bring home high grades and love you less when you make low ones.

Nothing could have prepared me for Jessica's sobering results:

> Over the past five years, I've asked this question to thousands of kids, ages 12 to 18, and the percentages still surprise me. Among middle-school children, about 80 percent believe that, yes, their parents truly love them more when they deliver high grades and less when they make low ones. In high school, the average is a little higher—about 90 percent.[4]

Although I tried to continue reading, I got stuck on that passage. I read it several times, opening myself up to the possibility that my daughter might raise her hand. Actually, I was quite certain she would. After acknowledging that difficult truth, I was able to continue reading.

Jessica went on to describe a critical concept called "outcome love." She quoted Jim Taylor, a psychologist who specializes in sports and parenting, who defines outcome love as, "a transaction in which parents bestow the reward of love in exchange for their children's success and withdraw that love as punishment for failures."

I thought about my distinctly different reactions to Natalie's high grades as opposed to her less-than-desirable ones, and I knew I had work to do. *But what?* Naturally, I turned to Google.

"Stop focusing on grades," I typed hastily in the search bar.

Article after article confirmed that placing high value on achievement and outcome (rather than effort) was detrimental to young people, leading to discontentment, stress, depression, and negative behaviors. Research encourages parents to relay the belief that abilities can be developed through dedication and hard work.

Two key passages from the articles stood out:

---

4. Jessica Lahey, "The Big Problem with Rewarding Kids for Good Grades and Punishing Them for Bad Ones," *The Washington Post*, August 29, 2018, https://www.washingtonpost.com/lifestyle/on-parenting/should-we-reward-our-kids-for-things-like-good-grades/2018/08/17/5910e896–9461–11e8–810c-5fa705927d54_story.html.

Focusing on the measurement of our performance reinforces what researcher Carol Dweck calls a fixed mindset. If students believe that how they perform at one moment in time exposes the limits of their potential rather than serving merely as a snapshot of where they are in the process of growing their abilities, feelings of struggle and uncertainty become threatening rather than an opportunity to grow.[5]

Place the value on your students' understanding. Use these recurrent assessments as a means for feedback and a way for your students to start to view their learning as a process through which they can practice, make mistakes, and learn from those mistakes to improve their understanding.[6]

I felt certain I could shift my focus from outcome to process, but there was something even more pressing that I knew I needed to address. I needed to change the first words I said to Natalie when her school day ended. Given my new knowledge, I realized my typical line of questioning was sending exactly the message that would make my daughter raise her hand during Jessica's talk.

Did you get any tests back?

Any grades today?

How did the quiz go?

What homework do you have tonight?

I thought about how I'd feel if my family were to greet me at the end of each workday with similar questions.

How many books did you sell today?

5. Joseph Holtgreive, "Too Smart to Fail?," Inside Higher Ed, August 16, 2016, https://www.insidehighered.com/views/2016/08/16/students-focus-too-much-grades-detriment-learning-essay.

6. Barbara A. Swartz, "Focus on Learning, Not Grades," National Council of Teachers of Mathematics, January 19, 2016, https://www.nctm.org/Publications/Mathematics-Teacher/Blog/Focus-on-Learning,-Not-Grades/.

What was the traffic on your website?

How many new subscribers did you get on your blog?

I realized that the questions I love most at the end of my day are:

How are you, Rachel?

How are you feeling about things?

I was quite certain my daughter felt similarly.

I immediately stopped asking Natalie academic-related questions the minute she walked in the door. Instead, my greeting addressed her well-being—the whole of her.

How are you feeling?

How did your day go?

And once I started really paying attention, it was easy to see that after her day is done, Natalie craves quiet alone time. After greeting her, I began waiting to converse with her until we were at the dinner table, in her room, or in the car. And when we did talk, I resisted the urge to ask about grades and other school related topics.

Instead of questioning her, I simply talked to her. I'd tell her something that had happened in the world or about my day. I'd ask for her opinion on recipes, weekend plans, music, fashion, travel. Within a few weeks, something quite hopeful happened. Natalie started sharing more with me. And honestly, it felt like she was breathing easier when I was near.

But the most unexpected part of this new approach was that I began receiving answers to all the school-related questions I used to ask. But instead of me asking, Natalie brought them up. She shared her assignment grades, including ones that were not quite where she wanted them to be. And when she did, I was prepared to offer a response that focused on her understanding of the material, on learning as a process, on the brain as a muscle that can grow with practice and exercise, on mistakes or low grades as a tiny snapshot of where she currently was in her learning process. My responses emphasized a growth mindset, which gives kids the best chance to create a thriving and fulfilling life as an adult.[7]

More often than not, my daughter already has some kind of plan for improvement—and while that plan might need tweaking or support, a new determination to emphasize growth over achievement motivated me to take my hands off the wheel, to accept that it wasn't my place to dictate and drive her plan. I understood that if it's *her* plan, there is a greater chance that whether or not it works, she will learn and grow. I understood that if I stood beside her rather than over her and looked for ways I could champion her efforts and progress, we'd both be better off.

But there was more, and it was so subtle I almost missed it. It was a stack of poetry books and inspirational quotes on the bedside table in our vacation rental.

Before we'd gone on fall break, I'd asked Natalie if she was going to bring her school books to read on our trip. "I do enough reading in school, Mom," was her response.

Instead of disagreeing or pushing, I listened to what she was saying and said, "Yes, you deserve a break."

One night during break, I noticed books on the bedside table. There were two poetry books and an inspirational quote book. She'd brought books after all, but they were books she'd brought to read for enjoyment, for enlightenment, for growth—not for a grade.

I sat on her bed, and I asked if the break was helping her relax and regroup after school. Natalie affirmed with a nod, but clearly her mind was on something else.

What she volunteered next surprised me. She told me that she had come to a decision about a male friendship; one that had teetered into that complicated gray area of relationships so difficult to understand, let alone define, in her current phase of life. She could

---

7. Scarlet Paolicchi, "The Growth Mindset for Kids—What It Is, Why It Is Important, and Change," *Family Focus Blog*, July 19, 2019, https://familyfocusblog.com/growth-mindset-for-kids/.

see that she was not being treated in a respectful manner and had made the decision to distance herself. Her decision was sound. It was healthy. It was smart. It revealed inherent wisdom that would serve her well as she grows.

This decision was not something she had to tell me—but she did. And that was significant. I knew my response would be important.

I did not say, "I'm proud of you," which I now see as an external judgment—a verdict on my child's performance or behavior. Instead, I said, "You're listening to your heart, and it knows what you need and deserve. I sure learn a lot from you. Thank you for sharing this with me."

I could tell by the look on Natalie's face that the affirmation was meaningful.

Suddenly, I knew why I'd been carrying around a particular quote as my latest anchor quote. This stunning declaration of unconditional love was written in 1912 by philanthropist Mary Elizabeth Haskell, in a letter to her friend, the poet Kahlil Gibran: "Nothing you become will disappoint me; I have no preconception that I'd like to see you be or do. I have no desire to foresee you, only to discover you. You can't disappoint me."

It seems like a tall order—impossible, even. Perhaps we've been conditioned to believe our job is to expect our loved ones to become everything we hope them to be, but what about who they *are*? And who *they* hope to become?

I'm quite certain the internal struggles I've had throughout most of my adult life would have been lessened if I had not lived in fear of disappointing people—if I had not based my worth on achievements, positive feedback, and external measures.

What if I'd known then what I know now: *that the opposite of outcome love is discovery love*? And that as I continue to seek to discover my child—rather than question, monitor, and expect things of her—I will also discover myself? I wonder how much peace and fulfillment we might grasp when we see life as an opportunity to grow, rather than an endeavor to accomplish, a list of expectations so high we are constantly left with disappointment.

I'm tired of living in disappointment. I'd much rather live in hopeful discovery.

To help, I've posted a daily intention on my kitchen cabinet, where I read it every morning:

Discovery Love Daily Intention

To be less focused on the marks you earn, so I can see the whole of your being.

To be less fixed on letter grades, so I can see the emerging lines of your story.

To be less set on my expectations, so I can see the magnitude of your possibilities.

Your achievements are only a sliver of who you are.
If I focus solely on the sliver,
I miss the highlights.
I miss the big picture.
I miss the tiny lines of poetry you've marked in yellow.
I miss the joyful lines around your eyes when you laugh.

As I love you with discovery of who you are,
I will discover love for myself that doesn't come with conditions.

Let's breathe easier today, my child.
No longer will we limit our worth
our light
our voice
our purpose
by outcome.

⊲⟡——— *Worthiness Waypoint 1* ———⟡⊳

MEANINGFUL MEASURES THAT MOTIVATE

Psychologist Carol Dweck defines motivation as "the love of learning, the love of challenge."[8] Her research has proven that motivation is often more important than initial ability in determining a person's success. Using Dweck's definition of motivation as a springboard, I reflected on the principles I'd learned during my teaching career that emphasize personal growth over external measures and that celebrate process over results. I identified six guidelines we can use to spark motivation in young people and prepare them to embark on the lifelong process of growth and self-improvement. Each guideline begins with an example of what we can say to tap into positive motivation.

1. *Focus on progress.* "Do you remember where you started? Well, I sure do. Let me tell you what I remember . . ."

   Helping young people avoid comparison to others and see how far they've come is a gift in both the short-term and in the long-term.

2. *Focus on emotional resilience.* "I noticed the way you handled that disappointment. It made me very proud."

   Handling disappointment with grace and maturity is a quality that will help your loved one stay optimistic and grow stronger in the face of letdown. When awards are presented

8. "Motivation," *SheKnows* (website), September 28, 2007, https://www.sheknows.com/parenting/articles/4084/motivation/.

and names are announced, it can be painful to not be on the receiving end of acknowledgement. When you see a young person deal with disappointment in a healthy way, recognize and affirm it.

3. ***Focus on positive traits and actions.*** "I really admire the way you helped your classmate with his reading struggles this year. Not many people would take the time to do that, but you did."

Traits such as kindness, generosity, and selflessness don't make report cards but are vital to a fulfilling and contented life. If the young person in your life exhibits such qualities, say something. Let him or her know those character traits matter to you and make a difference in the world.

4. ***Focus on strengths and gifts.*** "Your talent in _____ blows me away! I just love to see what you come up with!"

When you're handed a report card or assessment, fight the urge to address the negative marks first and instead recognize what went well. The same goes for end-of-the-year performances. Notice the good first.

5. ***Focus on empathy.*** "I really struggled during my first semester in chemistry. I felt like such a failure when everyone around me seemed to get it and I didn't."

Openly sharing your own struggles can make your loved one feel seen, understood, and hopeful that she or he will get through this.

6. ***Focus on a plan.*** "I can see this is not the outcome you hoped for. Let's talk about a plan to improve this situation."

Young people often struggle to get started on a task or rectify a situation because the first step seems too overwhelming. Helping them break down a large goal into small steps can produce a monumental shift from inaction to motion. Plus, knowing how to conquer an overwhelming task using this process is a lifelong tool that can be used to cultivate peaceful and productive purpose.

WORTHINESS THROUGH AFFIRMATION

One of my biggest regrets is not listening to my intuition. I can vividly recall several devastating incidents when my instincts warned me of danger or depletion, and I allowed outside opinion or other people's expectations to lead me into dangerous territory.

For that reason, I have had to work extra hard to surrender control when Natalie makes decisions for herself about academics, extracurricular activities, and her social life. My daughter's decisions are not always the same ones I would make, but they are hers. She owns them. She is ultimately responsible for them. With each stumble or triumph, she becomes wiser, stronger, more confident, and more capable of making better decisions.

As I've watched Natalie navigate her high school career, it's become increasingly clear that people often express comments, opinions, and recommendations that do not have her best interests in mind, nor do they align with her core values. This reality only reinforces how important it is for me to help her develop a strong internal guidance system and a positive self-concept that can overpower damaging voices of judgment, condemnation, pressure, and toxicity.

This is why I listen when she decides she needs to leave swim practice early to study for a test.

This is why I listen when she emails her coach or teacher to express a concern.

This is why I listen when she talks through what she needs to say to her teacher about a grade.

This is why I listen when she decides she's done enough for one day.

This is why I listen when she expresses discomfort with a particular person or social gathering.

This is why I listen when she says she is not hungry and does not feel like eating.

This is why I listen when she says she needs sleep or rest.

By listening, I show trust in my daughter's inner voice so she can learn to trust it herself.

There are many external and often unhealthy voices fighting for our attention in this world, and sometimes, as my own story proves, they fuel an internal voice that reflects some of these same negative and damaging messages. Fortunately, my daughter's internal voice seems perfectly calibrated with her best interests in mind. I'm not sure that would be true if I hadn't set out on this journey to change the context of our conversations, to learn how to truly listen rather than "fix," and most importantly, to trust her instincts—a practice that ultimately reinforces her muscle memory to do the same. Not only does her "inner protector" help establish lifesaving boundaries, but it knows her divine purpose extends far beyond grades, scores, appearance, status, and achievements. My daughter is coming to know her truth, who she is at her core. This knowledge will serve her well as she navigates life.

As we can all attest, the messages that come from our cultural influences, media platforms, and educational system can be so loud, so persistent, and so convincing that reinforcement is needed for each of us to follow our inner compass. It is in those times of doubt that we hope our kids will turn to us for the assurance they need—and that we will have the words to reset their compasses, too.

As the saying goes, old habits are in fact hard to break, so given my history with internal pressure, I often wondered what might come from my mouth if and when my kids turned to me in a moment of turmoil and self-doubt. I didn't have to wait long for an opportunity to find out.

One day, not very far into her first year of high school, I didn't have to practice my "wait to approach her" tactic to hear about her day—on this day, she sought me out. Visibly upset, Natalie described her day as "terrible." I immediately sat down as a way of nonverbally saying, "I am here. I am listening."

For nearly forty-five minutes, my emotionally reserved daughter unleashed her pain, stress, and disappointment. A mental red flag went up as Natalie expressed her views on our educational system's narrow definition of success and the pressure it put on kids who are working to achieve it. Her observations were similar to those expressed by a young man named Patrick Turner in the letters he wrote to school administrators, friends, and family before his death by suicide in 2018.

Patrick's letter to his school's administration began with, "The ongoing stress . . . has been inescapable," and "putting this much pressure on me has caused me to do what I do." In the letter to family, friends, and "whoever reads this," Patrick wrote, "One slip-up makes a kid feel like the smallest person in the world. You are looked at as a loser if you don't go to college or if you get a certain GPA or test score."[9]

I'd taken time to read through the heartfelt messages friends, family, and strangers from all over the world had written in Patrick's online obituary guestbook. I noticed how many teachers and parents indicated that Patrick's letters inspired them to talk about the increasing pressure children face in school, to look for ways to give their kids more time and space to just be kids, and to put more emphasis on empathy and community.

I didn't fully realize the extent to which Patrick had inspired me, too, until I sat listening to my own daughter echo some of the

9. David Whiting, "This 16-Year-Old California Boy's Suicide Letters Are a Cry for Help and a National Call for Change," *The Mercury News*, March 19, 2019, https://www.mercurynews.com/2018/03/19/this-16-year-olds-suicide-letters-are-a-cry-for-help-and-a-national-call-for-change/.

same concerns. Patrick's message led me to recognize an opportunity to forever affirm her internal compass and inherent value. Although I have it in me to be overly concerned with grades, honors classes, and college admissions, I chose to be more concerned with the emotional well-being and mental health of my child.

I looked into Natalie's worried eyes and said, "I love you, and I know you are doing the best you can."

She released a long-held breath, looking at me expectantly for more anchoring assurances.

I repeated my affirmation once more in hopes that she might say it to herself when the pressure began to mount once again—as I knew it would. Even as I spoke them, I prayed my next words would forever refute the damaging belief that academic achievement is the only route to a good life.

There is a great, big world outside the walls of your school and academic life; a world where skills like relating, managing, critical thinking, leadership, risk-taking, and initiative are needed. A world where attributes like compassion, integrity, perseverance, honesty, and ambition will be required if we are going to make important changes and breakthroughs happen. And there you will be, using your skills and your attributes to better the world. I will never let grades, scores, or reports let us lose sight of your purpose or potential.

And this girl, who is not much of a hugger, embraced me long enough that I had the pleasure of feeling her breathing return to normal.

Soon after our talk, Natalie took a big step out of her comfort zone and applied to be part of a learning trip to Rwanda—to the place her heart has called her to go since she was a young girl. Over the span of a month, Natalie worked through the ten short essay questions while learning as much as she could about the history of Rwanda and teaching herself basic phrases in Kinyarwanda.

While I listened to Natalie confidently explain the pros and cons of different vaccines used to prevent malaria, I thanked God for the timing of this opportunity. In a time when educational standards could have caused Natalie to doubt her worth and capability, she was instead embracing an opportunity to demonstrate her ability in tangible ways. My belief that this was a defining moment in her life was reinforced by the words of Patrick Cook-Deegan, founder of Project Wayfinder, an organization focused on helping people live more purposeful lives.

> Young people do not usually develop a specific purpose and then go become an expert in that thing. Rather, they are exposed to something new that helps them develop their own sense of purpose. In short, in most cases experiences lead to developing purpose, not the other way around. This is why summer experiences that introduce young people to new ways of seeing the world and themselves are so valuable. If young people are exposed from 15–19 years old to events to seek purpose, they will increasingly seek them out on their own until the end of their adolescence, giving them a higher likelihood of discovering their own sense of purpose.[10]

When Natalie presented her completed learning trip application to me, I asked her if I could read through her responses. One of the questions gave me pause: *Do you have any skills that could be useful on this trip?* In response, Natalie wrote, "I am a teenager, so I can listen and empower other young people with a personal connection."

Are there any life aspirations more valuable than connecting with other human beings to affirm their worth and offer belief in their ability to overcome?

---

10. Patrick Cook-Deegan, "How to Help Teens Find Purpose," *Greater Good Magazine*, April 16, 2015, https://greatergood.berkeley.edu/article/item/how_to_help_teens_find _purpose.

To listen for understanding.
To regard with love and care.
To bear witness to pain.
To empower through presence.
Such noble aspirations could save a life.
Such worthy pursuits could change the world.

Let's share this pressure-relieving, purpose-igniting good news with our kids while there is still time. We don't have to look far to find a stressed-out soul that needs to hear these truths:

Average grades do not mean you are an average person.
Below-average grades do not mean you will have a below-average life.
You are more than the grades you receive.
You are more than what you achieved today.
There is more than one path to success and prosperity.

Our greatest riches are not found in bank accounts, prestigious jobs, or shiny cars—they are found in one another.

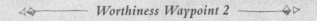

Worthiness Waypoint 2

EASING INTERNAL PRESSURE

The pressure our kids experience often comes from an internal source, as it did for me. Understanding this intense internal pressure to measure up can be difficult for parents who do not share the same emotional temperament. A friend of mine experienced this disconnect with her daughter and asked for my guidance. She explained that her daughter sets exceptionally high standards for herself, is self-critical, and is overly anxious about making mistakes. This young woman frequently comes home from school stressed out about the work she has to complete at night. My friend shared the suggestions she gives her daughter, which included, "Just relax . . . go outside and have fun . . . forget about it for a while."

My own perfectionist heart seized up as I recalled the many well-intentioned comments I received from people who worried about my stress level over the years: "Stop getting so stressed out," "It doesn't have to be perfect," "It will get done when it gets done." Such assurances are not helpful to people with perfectionistic tendencies and often exacerbate the problem because we then feel ashamed that we cannot just "let it go."

I gently acknowledged my friend's instinct to seek better ways to support her high-achieving child. I told her that figuring out how to validate and understand her daughter's perspective would probably feel more supportive and comforting to her child. To help, I shared part of Sandy Blackard's enlightening blog post, which was written to a parent struggling with how to support her perfectionist child:

> Bringing acceptance is always a good thing to do. You can start doing that right away by validating her need to be perfect, because to her it is extremely important, if not urgent, to be perfect.
>
> I know it may sound backwards, but from a perfectionist child's point of view, being told it is okay to mess up, show emotion and not care what her friends think, is telling her she is wrong to be herself, even if that is not your intention. . . .
>
> Here's why: The normal human reaction to being told you are wrong is to become defensive and prove that you are right. You are proving it to yourself as much as to the person who criticized you, tried to fix you, or told you that you were wrong. . . .

Acceptance is the missing element in shifting perfectionism from an anxiety-ridden malady to a gift of excellence. Once she knows it's okay to be the way she is (no matter what that is), she can naturally start to relax about it.[11]

I have witnessed proof of Sandy's statements in my own life. When I began to see the benefits of my high-achieving, extremely driven nature and began loving myself "as is," I felt the pressure inside me wane. That is when I began to say loving things to myself that I'd never said before:

- "It's good enough for today."
- "Getting it done is more important than getting it perfect."
- "That is not for me to worry about; my job is to focus only on the task at hand."
- "Just show up—that is all I have to do right now; I don't have to know how it's going to turn out."

When I say those words to my perfection-seeking, worry-filled heart, I feel pressure release, and I am no longer stuck in fear of not meeting a certain standard.

As for Natalie, my driven, conscientious, pursuer-of-dreams Wanderer, I have discovered that using these soul-building, pressure-relieving words makes all the difference:

- "Mistakes mean you are learning and taking brave risks."
- "You can have a few more minutes to work on your project. I see how important this is to you."

---

11. Sandy Blackard, "How to Help a Perfectionistic Child," *Medium* (blog), October 6, 2015, https://medium.com/@SandyBlackard/how-to-help -a-perfectionist-child-b068e75988e2.

- "You wanted it to be just right, didn't you?"
- "How can I help?"

By continuing to display authenticity, humanness, and self-acceptance during stressful situations and difficult seasons of life, I hope to alleviate some of the future pressure my high-achiever is bound to put on herself. Perhaps then we can both live out this hopeful truth: *The missteps of a messy, imperfect life are not something to be ashamed of or to avoid. They are necessary steps to becoming who we are meant to be.*

WORTHINESS THROUGH KNOWLEDGE

Near the end of Avery's elementary school career, the PTA requested a baby picture for the fifth-grade graduation party. I went through our digital photo albums and got lost for a bit—celebrating, remembering, rejoicing, and pausing.

The photo I lingered over longest was from her preschool graduation. I remember how difficult it was to stay composed that day. The sight of my ever-smiley child standing on stage in her pint-size cap and gown wrecked me. I blamed my strong emotional reaction on the songs the cherubic graduates sang about growing up and going to kindergarten. But the truth was, I was overcome with gratitude. Just months before Avery's graduation, I had faced a painful reality: I was missing my life—and with it, a chance to truly know my child.

With this awareness came the hope that by the time Avery walked across the stage at her high school graduation, I might really know her. It was the first time in a long while that I believed I could actually be there for her, both physically and emotionally, on that day and all the days to follow.

I began the journey to know Avery by paying attention. When she showed me who she was, I leaned in. This led to an exploration of responses that made her feel seen, heard, understood—or, simply put, *known*.

Here are just a few of my discoveries.

About Avery, I know . . .
She relishes her privacy when she changes clothes.
I stopped saying, "What's the big deal with me being here?"
Instead, I respected her boundaries.
And when I did, I saw peace on her face.

About Avery, I know . . .
She has a very low tolerance for pain.
I stopped saying, "Shake it off."
Instead, I empathized; I gave her loving support.
And when I did, I saw peace on her face.

About Avery, I know . . .
She is cautious when trying new things.
I stopped pushing her.
Instead, I offered patience and belief.
And when I did, I saw peace on her face.

The simple act of paying attention to the traits that made my daughter who she is boosted my desire to continue learning how to best love and support Avery. *By responding to her with words that expressed my acceptance of who she was at her core, I saw visible signs that she was feeling a new kind of peace for the first time.* What I couldn't see was that my words had given her the courage to begin making an important life decision for herself.

During a biennial family reunion on the Gulf Coast, eleven-year-old Avery made the decision to become a vegetarian. From my point of view, it all happened rather suddenly. One minute she was playing with ghost crabs at the beach, and the next, she was practically running from a restaurant where our extended family had gathered.

As plates of meat were set down around her, the color drained from her face. Avery leaned over and requested I go with her to the restroom. Once we rounded the corner, she grabbed my hand tightly. With pleading eyes, she said, "I want to become a vegetarian."

I did not know what to say or what to do, but that didn't matter.

She knew.

Avery knew herself.

From that day forward, Avery has been committed to this humane lifestyle and makes choices that feel right in her heart. She patiently answers questions from peers and is quite content eating alternatives to meat. Most of the time, other kids and adults are accepting of her choice, but occasionally, an issue will arise. One such issue happened at a friend's twelfth birthday party. The day after, I found Avery researching how the global food supply needs have influenced factory farming efforts. As they are tasked with increasing supply and controlling food costs, she read about some practices she deemed inhumane. When I asked if she was working on a school project, Avery explained that someone at the party had belittled her beliefs when she was eating a chickpea patty she'd brought from home.

"Why bother?" the child had asked Avery flippantly. "The chickens are going to get killed anyway."

Avery knew in her heart that her choice to abstain from meat *was* making a difference, but she wanted facts to support that belief.

I quickly retrieved the book, *Stuff Every Vegetarian Should Know*, that Natalie had given to Avery for Christmas. Thankfully, I'd just read it in an effort to support Avery's vegetarian lifestyle.

I knew exactly which page Avery needed to see. I opened to the most powerful page in the book: "One person's choice to go veg saves more than an animal a day—over 350 animals a year, of which at least 25 will be land animals such as cows, pigs, goats, and chickens. . . . If you stop eating meat at age 20 and keep at it . . . you will have saved over 1,000 land animals."

As I read the promising statistics to Avery, I saw that unmistakable look of peace. This information confirmed exactly what she felt in her heart.

I don't think it was any coincidence that a few hours later, Avery declared, "I think I am ready to get my new hamster."

It had been over a month since the unexpected death of her hamster, Mochi. Despite multiple stops into pet stores "just to look," Avery's response to every hamster she saw during that time was the same. "I'll know it when I see it," she'd say before turning away.

When she decided she was ready, we went back to one of the first pet stores we had visited. The same cute baby hamsters were still there. Avery had planned on getting a Syrian hamster like Mochi, but there were two teddy bear hamsters with beautiful coats and sweet faces.

Avery asked the store employee if she could see the brown-and-white one. The man hurriedly got the hamster out of the cage and ended up dropping her on the floor.

Judging by the height of the man, I cringed. I knew how dangerous it was for hamsters to fall even a few inches, let alone multiple feet! I looked at Avery's face, and it was colorless.

The salesperson was flustered and embarrassed; he quickly pointed to another hamster for Avery to consider.

"I will take her," Avery said pointing to the stunned little brown-and-white hamster. When the man didn't move, she repeated, "I want that one."

The bewildered employee then looked to me for direction.

"She knows," I said.

Avery looked up and smiled at me with relief, that distinct look of peace settling on her face.

Unlike her previous hamster, Kukui (named after the Hawaiian nut) is timid and does not like to be picked up (we certainly can't blame her for that!). Avery spends time talking to her, singing to her, and gently petting her back.

Kukui is the first thing Avery thinks about in the morning and the first thing she cares for when she comes home from school. She takes her job of cleaning, feeding, and nurturing very seriously.

As Kukui grew, so did the black markings on her ears.

"Look Mom!" Avery said pointing to Kukui's ear excitedly. "See the black fur on her ear? It's in the shape of a heart."

"I see the heart!" I marveled as my eyes shifted from the hamster to the young lady who loved the hamster.

At last, I could see more than just the peace on my daughter's face, I could see peace in her soul—and purpose.

To know who you are
and why you are on this earth
can change the trajectory of your life.

Rabbi Patricia Karlin-Neumann, Stanford's senior associate dean for religious life, describes purpose as an internal compass that serves both the self and the larger community. This echoes theologian Frederick Buechner's definition of purpose as described in *Wishful Thinking*, "The place where your deep gladness and the world's deep hunger meet."[12]

As I'm watching Avery's strong sense of self form before my eyes, I can attest that *purpose* could very well be the antidote for

---

12. Frederick Buechner, *Wishful Thinking: A Seeker's ABC*, revised edition (New York: HarperOne, 1993), 118.

feelings of anxiety, loneliness, sadness, and lack of fulfillment, all of which are at crisis levels for today's youth.

The author of a riveting article in *Palo Alto Weekly* summarizes the compelling thoughts of William Damon, Stanford School of Education professor and author of *The Path to Purpose*, who has spent years studying the stresses and demands put on young people by parents, schools, and the college admissions process.[13] "The biggest problem growing up today is not actually stress; it's meaninglessness," Damon says of his philosophy on purpose. "Working hard for something they didn't choose themselves, and don't believe in, is counterproductive to long-term health and fulfillment. It is simply not sustainable. A purposeful life, by contrast, can unleash tremendous energy, creativity, exhilaration and a deep satisfaction with efforts and accomplishments."

Whether it's playing her guitar for the elderly residents at the retirement home, talking up older cats to prospective adopters at the animal shelter, or making herself colorful meat-free lunches to take to school, I see Avery's dedication to these activities as beautiful illustrations of purpose as defined by Damon and his team of researchers: "a stable and generalized intention to accomplish something that is at the same time meaningful to the self and consequential for the world beyond the self."[14]

What cannot be emphasized enough is this: *These are not things I would have chosen for my child. She chooses far better than me—because she knows herself; she knows what she needs.* It was not always clear to me, but I now understand my job is to encourage her to trust and have faith in what she knows.

To choose your own path is the way to finding purpose and peace.

As Guides who listen and lean in when our children show

---

13. Teri Lobdell, "Getting Off the Treadmill," *Palo Alto Weekly*, November 2011, https://www.paloaltoonline.com/weekly/morguepdf/2011/2011_11_18.paw.section2.pdf.

14. William Damon, *The Path to Purpose: How Young People Can Find Their Calling in Life* (New York: Free Press, 2008), 36.

us who they are, we can serve as instruments of peace in which young people come to know themselves.

This is the path to self-acceptance . . .

So they can hear their calling, even when the world tries to drown it out.

So they are courageous in what they stand for, even when the world tries to push them down.

So they can grasp the true meaning of wealth, even when the world points to superficial standards of success.

So they possess an unshakable sense of peace, even when the world is stressful and unsteady.

"I will know it when I see it," Avery says, because she knows herself.

I can't help but feel excited about the moment she walks across the stage at her high school graduation. I'll lean over to the person next to me and whisper, "I know her . . . I know every beautifully unique detail about her. She's going to leave her mark—in the shape of a heart—on the world."

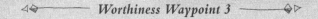

◁❧ ——— *Worthiness Waypoint 3* ——— ❧▷

HELPING KIDS PINPOINT WHAT'S IMPORTANT TO THEM

When Avery was in kindergarten, she asked me to read the words written in big, bold letters on her progress report. They said, "Distracted in large groups." But before she could feel one iota of failure or one ounce of shame, I came down on bended knee and said, "You are a Noticer. And the Noticers of the world are rare and beautiful gifts. I don't ever want you to stop noticing."

Embracing Avery's gift for noticing was a choice I made to reject the world's opinion of who Avery *should* be, and instead, embrace her for who God created her to be. Taking an unconventional path meant being the recipient of unwanted opinions, harsh judgments, and hurtful criticisms. It became clear to me that I could either use my time and energy to defend our decisions, or I could use them to nurture my daughter's heart-led choices that reflected her innermost truth and core values. I chose the latter and discovered two valuable pieces of wisdom in the process.

We can provide scaffolding for dreams and ambitions. Our kids have interests and passions that point them toward meaningful life goals, but they don't know how to reach those goals. As a result, they may make poor choices or improvise in unhealthy ways. This is the approach we took when Avery chose to become a vegetarian. Rather than throw in the towel when it seemed too hard to figure out and force her to go against her values, we met with a nutritionist. Avery learned how to live true to her heart while still taking care of her body.

During my author talks, young people often express how discouraging it feels to have their dreams diminished before they even have a chance to try. Although many adults believe it is their job to be realistic when dream jobs seem too far out of reach or not financially sound, there is no harm in hearing a young person out. Let's resist the urge to dismiss someone's plan just because there are some holes in it. Let's not declare a path is the wrong path just because someone gets a little off course. Let's choose to be advocates instead. Let's be the best Guides we can be; let's use our tools to fill the holes and our experience to help map their unknowns.

If the ideas expressed by the young people in your life are so far off in left field that you can't seem to get on board, perhaps there is a compromise. Somewhere in the middle of their dream and your wisdom and experience could be the best idea yet. By keeping an open mind—and open lines of communication—there is hope that you'll find middle ground.

We can ease the stress of the unknown. The admonition, "Find your purpose," is misleading and pressure-inducing. I have come to believe that we don't find our purpose; our purpose finds us. It happens when we identify something that feels important to us, and we show up—bravely, boldly, flawed, and full of hope, to do it—even if it doesn't make sense to anyone else.

One of the biggest sources of stress students express to me during my school visits is that they don't have any idea what they want to do with their lives. When people ask them what they want to be, the uneasiness of not knowing makes them feel like a failure.

While it is important for kids to develop their strengths and skills in school, it is also a time for them to discover what they love to do—and what they don't love to do—and to explore how their skills, strengths, and passion meet a need in the world. As Guides, it's our job to help kids uncover their callings by talking to them casually and non-judgmentally about their hopes for the future. Instead of asking, "What do you want to be?" try one of these alternatives.

- *What are you really good at? (If they cannot think of anything, it helps to ask, what do other people say you do that is special or helpful?)*
- *When do you feel the most alive? When do you feel the most at peace?*
- *What would be the absolute worst way to spend the rest of your life? Tell me why.*

- *What problem do you really want to solve? What skills do you currently have that are needed for this? What skills do you need to develop?*
- *What are your top five ingredients for a good life? What's a possible plan for grasping one of them?*

Consider this list of questions your invitation to help them see the possibility of what could be. And remember that our job is to listen; try not to interrupt or shut down ideas. The more we serve as sounding boards rather than dream crushers, the more thoughts we'll likely hear and the more input we'll likely be asked to give. By routinely listening—with an open mind and curious heart—to the ideas and dreams of young people, you set yourself apart from naysayers who deplete, discourage, and criticize. You become a soul-builder with whom the most sacred thoughts are shared. From there, they have a chance to be nurtured, develop their gifts, and become the world-changers they were born to be.

LIVE LOVE NOW REFLECTION: JUST BE

I sat completely still in the tiny recording studio, taking in the momentous occasion with every fiber of my being. Twelve-year-old Avery had set her life message to music and lyrics, and her song, *Just Be*, had already made an impact. Corey, Avery's guitar instructor, contacted me the evening she first played her song for him at practice. He said he was grappling with words to express how deeply her song had moved him. He said he'd choked up when telling his wife about the chorus. Corey felt strongly that *Just Be* needed to be accessible to anyone; that it could really resonate in our fast-paced, stressed-out world. Corey then offered to help Avery professionally record *Just Be* and make it accessible through various online streaming services.

After rehearsing for several months and getting her song just the way she wanted, Avery felt ready to record. After chatting with the producer and Corey about the process, she recorded the guitar track for the song. However, when it came time for the vocal track, something in her voice indicated she was not at ease. Even after several renditions, her voice remained tight and unnatural.

Remaining a quiet observer, I watched curiously as Corey, a singer-songwriter himself, motioned for Avery to come out of the recording booth. He then offered her this encouragement:

"When you are standing alone in a recording booth, staring at a wall, it's hard to remember there is a person who will connect to this song. On this next round, think of that person."

Corey looked down at his feet as if he was collecting himself. In a moment of vulnerability, he explained how *Just Be* provided him comfort as he was grieving the loss of his mom. He told Avery that as she was singing today, he was thinking about the birthday celebration his family was about to have for his dad that afternoon. It was his dad's first time celebrating without his beloved companion of thirty-four years.

"Even though this day is really hard, hearing you sing your song is giving me hope," Corey said.

Avery went back into the studio and sang the song again. The difference between the new vocal track and the previous ones was dramatic. The new track resounded with the full-of-life tone I hear when Avery performs for her nursing home friends, making lowered heads rise and arthritic hands clap.

This is the power of human connection, I thought. *Simply knowing you are making a difference can change the sound of your voice and the impact of your message.*

When we got in the car after the recording session, Avery's face had an unmistakable glow, the kind that comes when life unexpectedly opens its arms and spins you around until you fall over laughing.

After hearing Avery's happy thoughts about the experience, I marveled at the divine intervention that brought Corey, her special mentor, into her life, making this rare opportunity possible.

That's when Avery shared the never-heard-before story of how the song came to be.

"Corey taught me that chord—the one that runs through the song," Avery explained. "That chord that was so hard at first. My fingers didn't know how to make it sound good, but I just kept trying, even though it hurt. I think it was the challenge that made the song what it is."

My eyes immediately filled with tears as I made a critical connection. A decade ago, God had presented me with this precious Noticer to raise and nurture. I didn't know the first thing about loving this child, whose pace of life and inner fiber is in stark contrast to the pace and fiber of this world and, if I'm honest, to my world. I struggled at first; I inflicted pain at first; but I kept trying. I kept trying to know and accept her wholly and unconditionally. The result is imperfectly beautiful and unbreakably strong. Avery is her own person, and her message is exactly what the world needs now.

Just Be

Avery Stafford

Feel the vibrations in the strum,
Life's just the beat of a drum.
Right now, no one knows where we're going,
So let's just BE—

Cloudy skies, rain starts to fall,
Only Lord knows just who we are,
So let's just BE—

So what, if we're getting it done?
So what, if we're trying hard?
So what, if we're on the road to success?
All we can do is BE.

Be—
Be—

Feel the vibrations in the strum,
Life's just the beat of a drum.

As people have downloaded *Just Be* and allowed the lyrics to conjure personal meaning, they often want to tell Avery what her song means to them. Overwhelmingly, many agree that her song calls them to a place of peace—a place to stop striving, a place where *being* is enough, a place where *they* are enough.

Someday, perhaps sooner than later, I will tell Avery what *Just Be* means to me.

Each time I listen, I hear the divine whisper that saved me all those years ago, now embodied in her living anthem to the world.

Don't get ahead of yourself—stay right here.
Don't get lost in the past—stay right here.
Love in the moment.
This is where life is.

REFLECTION QUESTIONS

1. How do you typically experience pressure? Does it come from internal or external sources? In what ways, if any, does the pressure you feel affect the people you love? Describe one step you will take to relieve the pressure you are experiencing or cope with it in a healthy way.

2. Author Peggy O'Mara says, "The way we talk to our children becomes their inner voice." If this is true, what would the inner voice of your child sound like today? What changes, if any, would you like to make in the way you communicate with the young people in your life? Describe the specific changes and one small step you will take to begin.

3. While it is not in our power to give our kids a sense of purpose, we can give them space and opportunity so they can hear what they are being called to do. What are some ways you plan to give the young people in your life space and opportunity to explore their inner and outer world and discover what is meaningful to them? How will you set the example for a meaningful, heart-led life?

ONE WINDOW

By Natalie Stafford

One window is all I need,
To see what our world could become,
To know that we mustn't turn away,
To understand the pain of feeling invisible.

One window is all I need,
To experience real love,
To realize that everyone has insecurities.
To know that life will have hardships.

One window is all I need,
To find true friends,
To appreciate what I have.

One window is all I need to follow my heart,
To support others,
To notice the good in everyone.

> *One window is all I need*
> *To love as I have been loved.*
>
> —Natalie Stafford

I was around four years old when I started asking my mom for Talk Time. It was more like Question Time, because I always asked her to tell me something bad that had happened in the world that day. Somehow, I knew life was not always like the happy stories I read in picture books and saw in Disney movies. Although I couldn't explain it, I knew it was important to know real-life stories, even if they made me sad or scared.

My mom told me about the suffering in the world in ways I could understand. I am grateful she did this. Pretending suffering doesn't exist or ignoring it does not make it go away—it intensifies it. Knowing and understanding perspectives, cultures, and circumstances outside our own opens a window that calls us to seek answers to the most important questions of life.

At a very young age, my mom opened a window for me because I wanted to see the whole world, the beauty and the pain. I wanted to respond to it all with a loving heart and a desire to learn.

At age fourteen, that window opened wider than I could have imagined through a Learning Trip with a nonprofit organization called African Road whose mission is to use the richness of friendships to make way for sustainable growth led by local leaders and their communities in East Africa. Although I didn't tell anyone until months after the trip concluded, I'd actually been terrified to go to another continent. Being a bit of a germaphobe, my biggest fear was that I would get sick. But I felt certain that if I faced this fear and made the trip, it would give me the confidence to overcome future obstacles.

The moment I stepped off the bus onto the grounds of the

Togetherness Youth Cooperative in Gasogi, Rwanda, my fears immediately subsided; I was overcome with inexplicable peace. The Togetherness community, formed by Pastor Steven Turikunkiko in response to the cries of the children orphaned in the 1994 Rwandan Genocide, is now a community of 142 young adults and children. Through hard work, faith, and investment in sustainability from African Road, these young people have developed a community where healing, empowerment, and skill building happen on the soccer field, in the bakery, in the preschool, at the water well, and on the farm. One step at a time, they work together, moving from poverty and hunger to meeting their own needs and caring for each other and the neighbors around them.

Each day during my visit, I was greeted by the children's wide smiles and welcoming waves. One of my special young friends, Emmanuel, would walk right up to me, grab my hand, and lead me to a shady spot that overlooked the dirt soccer field, where we were joined by other children to draw, laugh, and just enjoy being together.

Although I replay many experiences from the Learning Trip in my mind, there is one moment that stands out from the rest. One morning, my mom and I were invited to play games with the preschool children. The teachers asked us to lead the Hokey Pokey. Because I am one who normally shies away from the limelight and does not feel comfortable singing or dancing in front of people, my response to their invitation shocked me. I actually hopped right up to join in. I looked at all the little faces around me and couldn't help but smile. As I spun around in circles and sang out loudly, the kids looked up at me and smiled and giggled. I became lost in that moment.

I'm quite certain I never knew pure and complete joy until that experience.

What created it? I can't be sure, but I believe it required stepping outside my comfort zone into unfamiliar territory with a completely open heart that allowed me to connect in the most pure and loving way. From that moment, a recurring question that had been in my mind changed from, *What do I want to do with my life?* to, *How is life calling me to hop up and participate with my whole being?*

Soon after the trip, summer break was over, and I went back to school. Although this enlightening experience didn't directly change anything back home, the suspicion that had been forming in my mind for a few years, maybe as far back as when I was four, was confirmed; it was clear to me that I would find life's most important questions and answers outside familiar territories and beyond my school walls.

In one particular class, the person sitting behind me was often reprimanded for not completing assignments. At first, I was upset, knowing how many of the young people I'd met on my trip would cherish that same educational opportunity. But as time went on and I experienced the pressures and expectations of high school, along with the requirements prescribed to be "successful," I felt compassion for that student.

I often wonder how things might change for young people if, instead of being backed into corners with questions like, "Why didn't you do your assignment?" we were given more opportunities to explore bigger questions.

Opportunities that would help us answer questions like:

Have you ever felt true joy?
Have you ever stood under a vast sky and felt small?
Have you ever held hands with a stranger who instantly felt like family?

What if, instead of pressure to answer questions like, "Do you have enough activities to build your resume?" we were challenged to open our minds to wonder and delight so that we could answer other questions?

Have you ever stood at a scenic lookout as long as your heart desired?
Have you ever looked fear in the face and said, "You can't stop me"?
Have you ever been so lost in a moment that every worry on your
mind was lifted?

I call questions like these Window Questions because they make me look at the world differently. They reveal how intelligence and wisdom are acquired through real-life experiences and relationships, as opposed to temporary retention of information for test-taking and busywork. Window Questions lead young people to think about how they can experience life's deepest joys. They also offer ways to find meaning when life seems hard or confusing.

I know this to be true because whenever I encounter a situation that causes me to doubt my capability or my worth, I open the journal I wrote in before and during my trip to Rwanda. These pages, now lined with red dirt, sweat, and a few tears, hold the beginnings of my purpose-discovery process. My journal is filled with fear-conquering quotes, beautiful memories, painful historic facts, children's drawings, and language unlike my own. I know the details of my trip will fade, and I know I can't yet grasp the whole big picture of my life, but I look at things through a new window because of these experiences. I wonder now about the unconventional path, asking myself how I can best contribute to our world and continue to learn as I go . . . and that's enough for me to see promise ahead.

If I could give the world one message, it would be this: *Open windows.* Dare to ask hard questions. Dare to respond in your truth. Dare to step out in courage. Dare to reach farther than you ever thought you could. Because the reality is, our best ideas and our bravest solutions to the world's big questions won't have a chance to surface if they're stifled by our worries, fears, expectations, or agendas. But they can be uncovered—by asking atypical questions; taking long walks with no destination; twirling tiny world maps hanging from a chain; going places we're afraid to go; looking into eyes filled with pain; and grasping small, dust-covered hands that take hold of your heart.

We simply cannot afford to let world-changing contributions become buried under a stack of things society says we "should do," suffocated by worry about failing before we even try or shut down by a standardized metric such as a poor letter grade. I would argue these outcomes are not failure of a human being but rather failure to open a window. One window could inspire even the most unlikely souls to hop up, put their whole selves in, and shake the world with hope.

May we all join in.

WE ARE OKAY

We hold hope and despair, one in each arm, and we cradle them close to our chest, because they both have something important to say at every moment.

—Kaitlin B. Curtice, *Glory Happening*

A few days before Natalie and I traveled to Rwanda, she hit her head on the side of the neighborhood pool. She'd been gliding along the pool floor with a friend and accidently swam right into the wall, resulting in a skinned nose and bruised forehead. Natalie laughed it off, but I worried. I thought getting her checked out by a medical professional would ease my angst, but even after that, I still worried that people we met along our travels would question her, perhaps causing us to be detained or separated. But in the end, the only people who noticed and inquired about Natalie's lacerations were the children we bonded with at the Togetherness Youth Cooperative.

At least once a day, a child would reach up and softly touch the bruised scab on Natalie's forehead, voicing concern in Kinyarwanda.

Using her hands, Natalie would entertainingly demonstrate

257

running into a wall and then say these assuring words, "I am okay. I am okay."

The children would smile back and breathe a sigh of relief. *She is okay.*

I didn't think about Natalie's words or that scab on her forehead again for six months after our trip. But the moment I did marked the end of an era of pain and the beginning of a message of hope.

It had been a difficult couple of weeks. Due to some frustrating and disheartening circumstances in my professional and personal life, I was operating with a heightened level of internal tension, a state capable of reducing me to old, unhealthy patterns. The hairline fractures in my mood and demeanor did not go unnoticed by my firstborn child, who seems to see me more clearly than anyone else. During that stressful period, Natalie observed symptoms of fear, vulnerability, and anxiety in me. She instinctively knew that, left untreated, those fractures would intensify to cracks and maybe even break, so she addressed them with love and concern.

What have you had to eat today, Mom?

Slow down; it's okay if we are a few minutes late.

You have done enough for today. Rest. Just rest, Mama.

Don't worry, Mom. The people who are meant to be there will be there.

Here, I can handle this; you go do what you need to do.

In addition to accepting Natalie's help and assurance, I anchored myself with peace, positivity, and awareness, all tools I've worked hard to acquire over the years. But the most powerful force that kept me motivated to show up fully and authentically in both the struggles and joys of each God-given day came from watching Natalie.

I marveled at the girl who set her morning alarm in time to make a healthy kale smoothie and then dove into a Big Mac after school.

I marveled at the way she didn't hesitate to reach out to a friend for help when she did not understand the new algebra concept.

I marveled at the way she accepted direct criticism from her coach after a swim meet. "If I thought I was doing everything right, I would not know how to improve," she said matter-of-factly as we walked through the parking lot.

I marveled at the way she laughed so hard at her mispronunciation of "Arkansas" that she nearly fell off her bed.

I marveled at the way she took breaks to read from her favorite poetry book during her study sessions.

One evening, I received disappointing news concerning a project I'd worked on for months, compounding my already heightened feelings of uncertainty and self-doubt. Refusing to let this setback pull me under, I followed the urge I felt to get outside and walk.

As I was leaving the house, I missed a step and fell hard on the garage floor.

"Natalie!" I cried out. "I fell!"

I heard my daughter scream and come running.

"I am okay. I am okay." I assured her before I knew if I really was. "I just . . . just don't want to be alone," I cried.

Natalie sat down on the steps and wrapped her arms around me. Her petite hand covered mine, and she rested her cheek against my face. I felt myself surrender completely to the present moment, and when I did, some pretty painful fears surfaced.

I was expecting my daughter to rush me to get up, like I did when she was young.

I was expecting her to ask how it happened and blame me, like I used to do when her sister fell.

I was expecting to endure the pain all alone.

But that is not what happened.

My child simply held me in connective silence.

When Natalie eventually pulled back to look me over under the florescent lights of the garage, I noticed the now permanent scar on her forehead.

Suddenly, the words Natalie said to the children came back to me.

"I am okay. I am okay."

But this time, the words were for me . . . for us.

She's okay.

I am okay, too.

While I huddled against my daughter on the cold floor of my garage, I experienced a profoundly healing realization.

I am not perfect; I am flawed. I make mistakes, and I have regrets, but I am trying, learning, growing. I am becoming the parent and person I always wanted to be—resilient, compassionate, honest, authentic, brave, wise, loving, and faithful—the kind of person I want my child to be. The kind of person she already is.

As I waited for the throbbing in my ankle to subside, the long-held guilt and remorse in my heart eased, too.

It's time, I thought.

It's time to stop focusing on what I didn't do then and focus on what I am doing differently now.

It's time to stop wondering if my worst moments are the ones that will stick with my child and focus on the best practices we're both learning together.

It's time to stop speculating on the damage I've done and focus on the tools I'm using to get unstuck when triggered.

It's time to stop wondering if my issues will wash out in the water and focus on the tears of redemption—the ones that fill my eyes when I watch my child swim, soar, live, and love.

She's okay.

And I am okay, too.

Neither of us expects the other one to be perfect; we simply expect that when we cry out in angst, pain, or fear, we will come to each other's side.

This is the kind of love I've always wanted to give.

This is the kind of love I've always wanted to receive.

This is the kind of love I've always wanted to leave as my legacy.

We are okay.

And with those three words, I got up slowly, gently putting weight on my ankle while wiping away my tears.

When I looked at the sky to determine if there was still time to walk before dusk, I saw the most beautiful phenomenon: both the moon and the sun were visible. This unusual spectacle spoke to me. It seemed to say, *Yes, there is still time. It's okay to feel caught between the dimension of today and tomorrow as we grow. You won't walk alone.*

I don't usually remember dates, but I will never forget this one.

On January 16, while on that very walk, I scribbled the beginnings of this book in the tiny notebook I carried with me.

"It's time," my Dreamer girl said.

As odd as it may sound, I felt peace knowing that my most painful truths might become someone's lifeline of hope.

The daily offerings of love and presence—no matter how imperfect or how small—are creating a better way.

The damaging patterns we are overcoming—not perfectly but whole-heartedly—are creating a better life.

Love doesn't have to be perfectly delivered to reach its recipient; it is the love that is given consistently—in times of struggle and in times of joy—that transforms us into who we're meant to be.

Let's keep reaching.

We are okay.

My Dreamer girl

Muncie, Indiana
1980

ACKNOWLEDGMENTS

"Be a lamp, or a lifeboat, or a ladder. Help someone's soul heal.
Walk out of your house like a shepherd."

—Rumi

I'll be honest. The beginning stages of this book-writing process were extremely difficult. In fact, fear convinced me I'd made a horrible mistake agreeing to write this book, and for several weeks, I wondered how I could get out of it. The problem was, I knew that in order to truly help people, I'd have to be completely vulnerable. I'd come to a point in my life where I knew facing and telling the truth was the only thing that made sense, yet, the prospect of documenting my most honest admissions for hours and hours each day felt like more than I could handle. And I worried that exposing these truths would open me up to criticism, judgment, and rejection when the book came into the world.

Simply put, I knew that writing *Live Love Now* meant I would have to navigate challenging territories I'd previously avoided, and I felt ill-equipped for the task.

After waking up in a cold sweat every night for nearly a month,

I called my agent and dear friend, Sandra Bishop. It was then that I dared to speak out loud the words that had been playing on repeat in my head.

"If I am going to do this, I cannot do it alone."

After declaring my fear to Sandra and hearing her priceless assurances and the reminder that I only needed to take it one moment at a time, I began asking and looking for writing re-inforcements in every way, shape, or form imaginable. Although I didn't know it at the time, the act of shedding light on my fear sparked a chain of empowering, miraculous encounters that made it possible for me to keep writing until I finished this book.

One of those encounters came in the form of a bench swing I stumbled on one evening while Avery was at her weekly gui-tar lesson. Although I'd walked around that same scenic area for many months, it wasn't until I was in the throes of writing *Live Love Now* that I discovered a rocky path that led to a beautiful, wooden swing.

When I first saw it, I thought I was dreaming—here was this suspended bench, smack dab in the middle of nowhere, showing up right when I needed peace and respite.

Ever since I was a young girl, swings have been places where I go to seek refuge. I'll never forget the day my mom told me that the tiny white kitten I'd chosen from the litter of seven had not survived. I tore out of the house to the backyard swing where I remained for hours, swaying back and forth, mourning my little Butterball. I vividly remember how all at once, my tears stopped, and I felt an unexplainable peace. My four-year-old heart and mind suddenly believed it would be possible to love the orange kitten just as much as the one I'd chosen myself. And I did—for fourteen glorious years, I loved Tigger more than humanly possible.

Decades later, while the process of writing this book had me mourning things I'd lost, this familiar source of comfort appeared in my path. Each Wednesday evening, after delivering Avery to her lesson, I would actually run down the rocky trail, so I'd have as much time as possible to swing, breathe, listen, and pray.

While there, I also smiled at passersby and admired pups on leashes with happy, pink tongues. But most of all, I imagined you, the reader of my book, turning to a specific page in this book and feeling seen and understood by the truths written there.

Each week, while I swayed back and forth in rhythmic peace, imagining you holding these hope-filled pages in your hands, my fear got smaller and my courage grew stronger. Each visit to the swing increased my belief that I was to be a messenger, and not to worry, because I'd be equipped for the task.

I learned to have faith that not only would there be swings along the journey for healing my soul, there would also be lamps, lifeboats, and ladders, all of which would enable the words in this book to reach you.

Thank you, my lamps . . . for illuminating my path, checking my progress, fueling my belief when I was running on empty, and for always leaving the light on for me.

Kerry Foreman
Jennifer Harbour
Cindy Carr
Britt Nixon
Maggie Muschara
Lynn Clark
Megan Haralson
Carrie Brewer
Jeanne Lowe
Rachael Stephens
Julia Fehrenbacher
Diane Chaniewski
Suzanne Guy

Nancy Janas
Mary Largent
Carrie Wertheimer
Alexandra Rosas
Patti and Bob Petersen
Stacie, Jon, Sam, Evan, and Kate Oliver
Ben Stafford
My Soul Shift Family
The Hands Free Revolution Community

Thank you, my ladders . . . for propelling me over difficult obstacles, elevating my words and experiences to new heights, and leading me to extraordinary people, places, and parts of myself that without you, I'd never know.

Kelly Dispennette
Krystle Cobran
Darrell Vesterfelt
Carolyn McCready
Kaitlin Curtice
Katrina Willis
Becky Gensel
Corey Shores
Sandy Blackard
Alice Kajoina
Kellie McIntyre
Harmony Harkema
Shannon Brooks
Amy Paulson
Tanya Fenner
Noah Kahan
Kelly Bean and friends at African Road

Alicia Kasen, Trinity McFadden, Jennifer VerHage, and the
    entire Zondervan team
Steven Turikunkiko and the Togetherness Youth Cooperative
Kristy Grieco and friends at All About Cats
John Abel and the A.G. Rhodes Nursing Home residents

Thank you, my lifeboats . . . for never letting go of my hand.
You are my oxygen; my true north; my constant source of comfort, hope, belief, and inspiration. You are my home, and this book is a result of your steadfast love and support.

Scott Stafford
Natalie and Avery Stafford
Harry and Delpha Macy
Rebecca Macy
Sandra Bishop
Banjo Stafford

Thank you, God. I knew the precise moment you joined me
on the rusty swing set behind my Iowa home, when you showed
me how I could hear you in the wind, the trees, and in my own
beating heart when I placed my small, bare feet upon the grass.
It was there, when I lost my beloved kitten, that you gave me the
assurance that would sustain me time and time again: We may
not get the life we picked, but we can come to cherish it just as
much—perhaps even more—than the one we would have chosen
for ourselves.

PATRICK'S PURPOSE

The Patrick's Purpose Foundation was created to honor Patrick Turner's legacy and character through making the positive changes that he wished for. The foundation aims to promote mental wellness in schools and create a student-driven culture of kindness through educational programs and initiatives. Additionally, they award scholarships to selected students who attend a vocational school or community college. To learn more, go to https://www.patrickspurposefoundation.org.

AFRICAN ROAD

African Road is a nonprofit organization working to lift entire communities out of extreme poverty. They partner with local Changemakers in Burundi, Kenya, Rwanda, and Tanzania through collaborative project development and strategic funding. The work of African Road is not charity or aid—it is empowerment for transformation, fueled by friendship and stories of hope. African Road focuses on integrity, grit, and sustainability. This is the change East Africa desperately needs. To learn more, go to https://www.africanroad.org.

Only Love Today

Reminders to Breathe More, Stress Less, and Choose Love

Rachel Macy Stafford

New York Times bestselling author Rachel Macy Stafford shares simple words of inspiration each day to help you find hope and encouragement amidst life's challenges.

Millions of Stafford's fans from her blog and her books find hope, challenge, and inspiration through her poetic and powerful short pieces on her blog. *Only Love Today* brings these pieces and many new, original entries together in a beautiful book based around the four seasons.

From finding daily surrender in the autumn and daily hope in the winter, to daily bloom and daily spark in the spring and summer, you will always find fresh beautiful words for your day.

With a flexible, non-dated structure, *Only Love Today* is perfect to pick up at any time of the year to find strength and vision for a new and more connected way to live.

Available in stores and online!